The

INSIDE PASSAGE

TRAVELER

Getting Around
In Southeastern Alaska

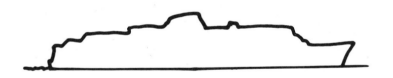

By: Ellen Searby

Windham Bay Press
Juneau, Alaska

Eldred Rock Lighthouse in Lynn Canal, between Juneau and Haines.

Front Cover: *Columbia* cruises the Inside Passage on a calendar-photo day.

Back Cover: Mendenhall Glacier on a bright fall day.

Windham Bay Press
Box 1332, Juneau, Alaska 99802

ISBN 0-9605526-6-9   ISSN 0736-9298
Printed in the USA   Key title: Inside Passage Traveler

FOREWORD FOR 1985-86

After three summers as a U.S. Forest Service shipboard naturalist, answering (or trying to answer) all the questions that over 30,000 people aboard the Alaska ferries could ask, I thought it would be worthwhile to put the information into book form. Many questions concerned not forest and wildlife but towns, routes and ferries.

I hope that knowing what is in Southeastern Alaska, how the ferry system works, and how you can make best use of it will help you to have a really great trip.

In this eighth edition of the book, I have used the information and suggestions some of you have provided as well as what I have gathered since 1978 as a member of the ferry crew. Please note that all prices are the anticipated 1985 summer rates, except as noted.

Please send suggestions you think I should cover and information you find useful to Windham Bay Press, Box 1332, Juneau, Alaska 99802. I apologise for having very little time for answering questions and no time to plan readers' trips, but my 24 hour day isn't long enough.

Many thanks again to all the nice people in towns, visitors' bureaus, the ferry system, and passengers on the ships who helped me gather the current information we all needed.

Have a wonderful time! I hope the sun shines for you!

Ellen Searby

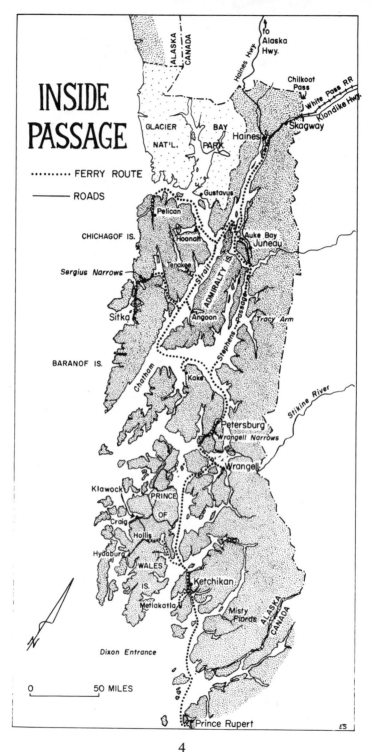

INSIDE PASSAGE

········· FERRY ROUTE

———— ROADS

ALASKA / CANADA

to Alaska Hwy.

Haines Hwy.

Chilkoot Pass

White Pass RR

Klondike Hwy.

GLACIER BAY NAT'L. PARK

Haines

Skagway

Gustavus

Pelican

CHICHAGOF IS.

Hoonah

Auke Bay

Juneau

Tenakee

Sergius Narrows

Strait

ADMIRALTY IS.

Sitka

Angoon

Tracy Arm

Stephens Passage

BARANOF IS.

Chatham

Kake

Stikine River

Petersburg

Wrangell Narrows

Wrangell

Klawock

PRINCE OF WALES IS.

Craig

Hollis

Hydaburg

Ketchikan

Metlakatla

Misty Fiords

ALASKA / CANADA

Dixon Entrance

0   50 MILES

N

Prince Rupert

ES

TABLE OF CONTENTS

TABLES AND MAPS

TABLE 1

AVERAGE PRECIPITATION BY MONTH
(in inches)

	KETCHIKAN	JUNEAU
January	12.79	4.94
February	13.35	7.10
March	13.46	6.17
April	13.15	6.43
May	9.70	6.23
June	7.74	3.58
July	7.50	5.34
August	12.17	7.58
September	12.84	9.59
October	24.96	13.01
November	17.90	10.02
December	18.83	10.11
Annual	164.39" (over 13 ft!)	90.10"

AVERAGE TEMPERATURE BY MONTH
(Degrees Fahrenheit)

	KETCHIKAN	JUNEAU
January	34.0	25.8
February	36.5	30.9
March	37.7	33.9
April	43.4	41.0
May	50.3	48.9
June	54.7	55.4
July	58.7	58.9
August	58.7	57.0
September	54.4	51.8
October	47.3	47.3
November	40.7	37.3
December	37.2	32.1

Good luck picking the weather for your trip!

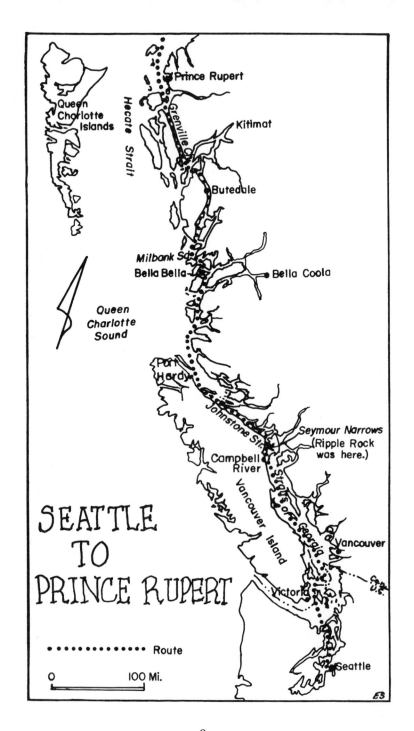

Prince Rupert

Queen
Charlotte
Islands

Hecate Strait

Grenville

Kitimat

Butedale

Milbank Sd.

Bella Bella

Bella Coola

Queen
Charlotte
Sound

Port
Hardy

Johnstone Str.

Seymour Narrows
(Ripple Rock
was here.)

Campbell
River

Vancouver Island

Strait of Georgia

Vancouver

SEATTLE
TO
PRINCE RUPERT

Victoria

Seattle

• • • • • • • • • •   Route

0   100 Mi.

E3

Patterson and Muddy River Glaciers north of Petersburg.

SOUTHEASTERN ALASKA

Welcome to Southeastern Alaska, the northern Inside Passage, the Alaska Marine Highway, and the Tongass National Forest. Here are hundred of miles of sheltered waterways, islands, mountains, glaciers, fiords, and thick spruce-hemlock forests— with all the wildlife that can live on land and sea. Scattered throughout an area larger than Massachusetts, there are 7 towns and 10 villages, with fewer than 60,000 people. That leaves a lot of uncrowded space and clean air!

The scenery and climate are comparable to the coast of Norway, but much closer to home. The Inside Passage is one of few places on earth where you can be among mountains and glaciers with no physical exertion, keeping your cardiovascular system at sea level, and without even getting seasick. For the more athletic, there are waterways to kayak, mountains to climb, and the Chilkoot Trail to hike.

There are two kinds of weather here: the one that makes the area what it is, and the one you hoped it would be. Rain and clouds are common, but the climate does get drier as you head north. The sunny days are worth it all. June and July are the driest months, while October is the wettest. Do bring rain gear so you can get out and explore, no matter what the weather.

Most of the towns in Southeastern Alaska are on islands, with water that is often 1,000 feet deep between them. There are no roads connecting the main towns, as the expense per capita is simply too great. Water can be an obstacle, or it can be a well-marked freeway, built by nature and maintained at small cost by tides and the Coast Guard.

Alaska has used her natural waterways to provide a transportation system between the people of "Southeastern," as it is often called (and you thought this was the northwest!), and the rest of the state, as well as the "lower 48." Using ships instead of buses and trucks, Alaska has developed the most enjoyable public transit system in the world—the Alaska Marine Highway.

The *Chilkat*, shuttling between Ketchikan and the Tsimshian village of Metlakata, is the first Alaska ferry, bought by the new state in 1959.

THE ALASKA MARINE HIGHWAY
What It Is

The Alaska Marine Highway is Alaska's answer to surface transportation for people and vehicles on the Southeastern Alaska coast. People traveling to or from Southeastern Alaska drive, but between its towns they ride the ferries (your fellow passengers may include the circus, the carnival, scout troops, and the little league teams).

The world's longest ferry route, 1,142 statute miles in Southeastern Alaska, Canada, and Puget Sound, began service in 1963 with 3 new ships named for Alaskan glaciers: *Malaspina*, *Taku*, and *Matanuska*. The *Columbia*, the largest and fastest of the fleet, was added for the Seattle run in 1974. Ferries sail from Seattle and Prince Rupert, B.C., north to Skagway several times weekly, stopping at Ketchikan, Wrangell, Petersburg, Sitka, Juneau, and Haines.

The *LeConte*, *Aurora*, and *Chilkat*, which are smaller ferries, provide local "bus" service to Hoonah, Pelican, Tenakee Springs, Angoon, Kake, Hollis, and Metlakatla, as well as to several of the mainline ports.

Serving most of the towns in Southeastern Alaska, these ferries run through narrow passages close to shore, such as Wrangell Narrows and Peril Strait, where passengers watch bald eagles on their nests, and sometimes bear and deer on shore. The ferries run all year, though they make fewer trips in the winter as the ships take turns in the shipyard for annual maintenance.

Two additional ships, the *Tustamena* and the *Bartlett*, also operated by the Alaska Marine Highway System, serve ports in South Central and Southwestern Alaska, including Kodiak Island and the Aleutian Chain. Their routes do *not* connect with those of the Southeastern ships. They are discussed briefly in the Southwestern section at the end of this book.

The Ships

The gleaming blue-and-white ships of the Alaska ferry fleet may change your image of "state ferry." Despite running continuously, they are nearly spotless, thanks to the stewards and deck crew.

On each of the four main ships you will find cabins with two or four berths (some with three or five berths on *Matanuska*), a cafeteria, a cocktail lounge, a gift shop, and a forward observation lounge. All have closed-circuit TV on which films are played several times a day. There is a reclining lounge with airline-type chairs for sleeping if you don't have a cabin, plus free showers (bring your own soap and towel) and baggage lockers. Towels, pillows and blankets can be rented with a deposit.

The car deck holds over 100 standard cars, or their equivalent in vans and campers. You may go to your vehicle while the ferry is in port, or with a crew escort during deck calls, but you may not, under Coast Guard regulations, stay on the car deck while the ship is under way. If you really need something from your vehicle which can't wait until the next port or car deck call, you can ask at the purser's counter for an escort to the car deck. Pets must remain on the car deck in vehicles or secure containers provided by the owners.

All Southeastern ferries except the *Chilkat* have glassed solariums on the bridge deck stern (upper deck). These are roofed, somewhat heated, and open to the rear with a clear view of the scenery and wildlife. The clean Alaskan air is a real treat. You can lounge in the solarium, or sleep there in dry comfort if you bring a good sleeping bag, a plastic sheet or tarp, and perhaps a foam pad. A limited number of chaise-lounges are provided. On warm days passengers sun-bathe and children sometimes fly kites.

Tracy Arm, south of Juneau, is a scenic fiord with many waterfalls.

The *Columbia, Matanuska, Taku,* and *Malaspina* have passenger elevators. All are on the car deck forward. Aboard the other ships, seamen will assist handicapped passengers to the boat deck, where the lounges and food are found. There is a powered baggage cart that hauls baggage between the car deck and the terminal building. Passengers are responsible for all other handling of their baggage. It is convenient to have what you will need en route packed separately to bring to upper decks (including medicines, cameras, film, binoculars, etc.) so you can leave the rest in your vehicle. It should not be left on the baggage cart unless you are getting off at the next port.

Many passengers bring snack-food with them, and there are several places on the ships where "brown-bagging" is allowed, including the solarium. Fire regulations do not allow cooking aboard ship. The steward's deparment will heat baby bottles and fill thermoses (if you bring them), so you can have hot coffee in your cabin. They will also heat special diets if you bring them, but are not equipped to provide them.

If you need any help or information, you can ask those incredibly patient pursers (on the cabin deck), the watchmen and other members of the crew, and in the summer, the U.S. Forest Service naturalist.

On the *LeConte*, *Aurora*, and *Chilkat* there are no cabins though the *LeConte* and *Aurora* have free showers. They usually serve shorter distances between ports, as they have more stops. It is possible, however, to ride from Skagway to Petersburg on the *LeConte*, and from Prince Rupert to Petersburg on the *Aurora* (leaving Tuesday), so be prepared if you are riding on those runs. Both ships do have solariums. The *LeConte* and *Aurora* also have small cafeterias and cocktail lounges—they are really just miniatures of the big ships. There is no food service on the *Chilkat* in summer.

"Make her fast." A seaman adds more turns of the line on the ferry's stern winch at Wrangell.

How The Ferry System Works

The Alaska Marine Highway is a public transit system (think of a marine bus), not a cruise ship fleet. Its routine is designed to provide the best possible service to an otherwise inaccessible area, which just happens to have fantastic scenery and wildlife. The terminals are usually not downtown, and may even be several miles away. The location of each terminal, and what is within walking distance from it, will be discussed separately for each port.

A ferry may dock at a civilized hour, allowing you to see the town and its surroundings, or it may dock and depart in the middle of the night. This you can discover from the ferry schedule. Stop-overs are the solution to untimely landings, and will be discussed in the next section. Ferry schedules for summer are available in December, and for winter, by the end of August. Supplementary information is also provided. Early reservations (January) are advised for vehicle and cabin space, especially during the summer.

The Marine Highway is not quite as predictable as the Los Angeles Freeway. Fog may slow ferries, and reliable as they are, ships do occasionally need repair. When there is a capacity load aboard the car deck, loading takes longer, and sometimes a ship misses the tide. This doesn't happen often, but you will be more relaxed if you don't plan tight air or rail connections, especially at Prince Rupert and Ketchikan, where the airports are on other islands that must be reached by boat and bus. As there are several areas of tide constraint on the Seattle run, it's best to allow at least 8 hours for southbound air and rail connections in Seattle. If you allow 6 to 12 hours at the Skagway end, you will have time to see the town and not miss a bus if the ship is late.

Tides are often over 20 feet. Your ship requires at least 5 feet of water under her keel in Wrangell Narrows, and slack water at the tide change when she goes through Sergius Narrows near Sitka. The captain will adjust the schedule as much as he has to for these conditions, making up time at port stops to get back on the printed schedule. Occasionally these adjustments allow enough time at an otherwise short stop, like Wrangell or Petersburg, for a walk to town or a visit to a museum. Making up time from port stops may leave no time for exploring some towns. If you really want to see a town, plan a stopover.

Because docks are usually outside of town and the ships often dock outside of closing hours, shopping enroute is often difficult. In Ketchikan there is a shopping center 1¼ miles toward town. The Sitka stop is also long enough, but shopping may mean not going on a sightseeing tour. The gift shops on the ships have some supplies and toiletries. It is well to be supplied with what you will need enroute, including supplies for children's activities if you are traveling with children.

Traffic lines up for the ferry at Sitka.

RESERVATIONS AND PEAK SEASONS

At these times the cabin and car decks are full, necessitating either reservations for those facilities, or considerable flexibility in your schedule. Reservations for cabin or car space are always advisable. For summer travel, these reservations should be made by January 10. Being "on standby" with a vehicle can mean getting up at 3 a.m. to see if you are going to get dropped off at some port to wait for the next day's ship. Even in peak season there is often vehicle space available north of Ketchikan though staterooms are usually full. If you don't have a stateroom but want one, sign the purser's wait list as soon as you board the ship. In Seattle the list is available for signing at the purser's hut at the head of the loading ramp when passenger loading starts. Any available rooms are sold in the order of the list.

Recently the ferry system began accepting applications for reservations any time they are sent in, acting on them in the order received starting the first working day in January. For example, in May 1985 you could send in an application for reservations on the ferry for July 1986, and it would be held until the first working day in January 1986, but would be acted upon before those received in November 1985. Many summer sailings are completely filled by the end of the first week in January.

Your reservation request should include your ports of embarkation and debarkation, names of all members of your group, ages of children under 12 years at time of trip, width, height, and length including any hitch of vehicle, mailing address and telephone number, alternate dates if cabin or vehicle space isn't available, date you will be leaving home. Fare must be paid in full at least 45 days before sailing or the reservation will be cancelled. Personal checks are accepted only on banks within Alaska.

A toll-free reservation phone system has been installed in Juneau with additional agents for reservations and information. From other states, dial 1-800-544-2251. From within Alaska, it's 1-800-551-7185. The system operates 10-12 hours a day, so you may get through outside normal working hours in January.

Demand for ferry transportation to and from Seattle greatly exceeds the capacity of the ferry system, especially during peak season. Without building additional ships that aren't needed much of the year, the ferry system cannot provide all the state-room and vehicle space people want. There is some luck as well as early action required in getting those reservations. The alternative (and the pleasure of riding less crowded ships) is finding another way to or from Prince Rupert, British Columbia, using highway, rail, air, or British Columbia ferry transportation. These are discussed under Prince Rupert and "Driving the Alaska Marine Highway Your Way," the next section. All passengers, including walk-ons, do need reservations to or from Seattle.

Chief Mate Raoul Ornelas stands beside the famous Green Tortoise camper bus as it leaves the *Taku* in Prince Rupert.

Traffic flow during summer varies as follows, though the trend is for a longer heavy flow in the fall each year:

NORTHBOUND: Increasing traffic through June, peaking in mid-July, then tapering off.

SOUTHBOUND: Increasing the second week of July, and remaining heavy until Labor Day when it drops off rapidly.

Many people avoid crowds and improve their chances of getting cabin and vehicle reservations, even in summer, by going north in May or early June, returning south in late June or early July. Others go north in August and return after Labor Day.

May usually has better weather than late September or October, as well as longer daylight hours. Plane, charter boat, and lodge schedules in Glacier Bay are geared to a summer season from late May to late September. Many other activities in towns, such as some play performances, happen only in summer. Ferry service increases in frequency during May as ships end winter maintenance. Life aboard ship is more relaxed with seats available and little waiting in cafeterias during spring.

Even in summer, the smaller ferries *LeConte*, *Aurora* and *Chilkat*, are generally less crowded than the mainliners.

The weekends of the Little Norway Festival in Petersburg, May 17-19, 1985, and of the Southeast Alaska Fair in Haines, August 16-18, 1985, fill the ships between Petersburg, Haines and Juneau, even for walk-on passengers. Ferries also become crowded when bridges wash out and mud blocks the Alaska or Cassiar Highways. If you can plan around the foreseeable peak periods, you will find the ships less crowded and more relaxing. A fringe benefit: more of the passengers will be Alaskans, with much to tell about their home. Rates for passengers and vehicles—though not for cabins—are lower between October 1 and April 30.

During peak season, you and your fellow passengers will appreciate any courtesy in sharing seats, especially near windows. There are no reserved seats on the ships, so they cannot be held while you eat or sleep somewhere else. You may want to bring a foam or air cushion for sitting on deck on nice days. If you smoke, please observe the no smoking areas, and think a second time before lighting a cigar or pipe in enclosed parts of the ship.

In recent years increasing numbers of passengers have been pitching freestanding tents on the stern decks. Presently (spring 1985) there is no restriction on this. However, in summer these tents take more than one or two people's share of the available space. They also block others' view of the scenery everyone came for. Cooking anywhere on the ship except by the crew in the galley, including inside tents, is prohibited by Coast Guard regulations.

The British Columbia ferry unloads at a dock adjacent to the Alaska ferry in Prince Rupert.

TIME

North of the Alaska-Canada border in Dixon Entrance, your route is in the Alaska Time Zone, one hour west of the Pacific Time Zone. Blessed with a state government which doesn't believe in longitude, Alaska in 1983 persuaded the federal government to reduce its four time zones to two. The state is on Daylight Savings when the rest of the nation is.

All ferries operate on Alaska Time even when in Canada or Washington. You change time zones (set your watch back 1 hour) when you board the ship at Pier 48. From there you have a leisurely few days to get over jet lag!

During May, June, and July Southeast Alaska has very long hours of daylight though not the midnight sun that shines farther north. There is nearly an hour more daylight at the north end of Southeastern Alaska than at the south during these months. The situation is reversed in winter as daylight in Juneau is about seven hours a day. In summer the sun is up over 19 hours a day and much of the night is twilight.

Location	Date	Sunrise	Sunset	Daylight Hours
Juneau	June 20	3:51 a.m.	10:09 p.m.	18
	Aug. 20	5:30 a.m.	8:31 p.m.	15
	Dec. 20	7:46 a.m.	2:07 p.m.	6
Prince Rupert	June 20	4:30 a.m.	9:30 p.m.	17
	Aug. 20	6:00 a.m.	8:00 p.m.	14
Seattle	June 20	5:00 a.m.	9:00 p.m.	16
	Aug. 20	6:15 a.m.	7:20 p.m.	13

Approximate times of sunset and sunrise with hours of daylight.

TABLE 2

MILEAGE AND SAILING TIME ON THE ALASKA MARINE HIGHWAY FROM SEATTLE

Position	Statute Miles		Hours (at 17 knots)
Port Townsend	45.4		2.6
Seymour Narrows (Campbell River is town just to south)	236		12.9
Kelsey Bay	274		15.4
Queen Charlotte Sound (south end)	369		20.3
Queen Charlotte Sound (north end)	398		21.8
Bella Bella	458		25.2
Milbanke Sound (south end)	476	(approx.)	26.2
Milbanke Sound (north end)	492	(approx.)	27
Boat Bluff	507		27.8
Butedale	544		29.8
Prince Rupert	632	(approx.)	34

Sailing Route	Statute Miles		Time (at 17 knots)
Ketchikan-Seattle (Active)*	747.8		38 hrs. 12 mins.
Ketchikan-Seattle (Rosario)*	752.9		39 hrs. 30 mins.
Ketchikan-Prince Rupert	105.8		6 hrs.
Ketchikan-Wrangell	99.7		5 hrs. 30 mins.
Wrangell-Petersburg	46.0		3 hrs.
Petersburg-Juneau	124.0		6 hrs. 45 mins.
Juneau-Haines	103.8		5 hrs. 40 mins.
Haines-Skagway	14.4		1 hr.
Auke Bay-Haines	77.6		4 hrs. 15 mins.
Sitka-Auke Bay	151.8		8 hrs. 15 mins.
Petersburg-Sitka	176.0		10 hrs.
Seattle-Skagway Direct	1142.0	(approx.)	60 hrs.
Seattle-Skagway via Sitka	1318.4	(approx.)	76 hrs.
Prince Rupert-Skagway Direct	493.7	(approx.)	32 hrs.
Prince Rupert-Skagway via Sitka	671.3	(approx.)	51 hrs.
Haines-Anchorage	803		
Haines-Fairbanks	669		

All ships reduce their speed in narrows and congested areas.

Cruise speeds: *Columbia*, 18 knots; *Malaspina, Matanuska,* and *Taku,* 16½ knots; *LeConte* and *Aurora*, 15 knots.

A knot is 1 nautical mile per hour, 1.15 statute miles. Since the *Columbia* is faster, its sailing times are less than shown. Ships on the Seattle run do not stop at Prince Rupert.

*Alternate routes at north end of Puget Sound. Choice varies with ship, traffic, and weather.

TABLE 3

RATES ON THE ALASKA MARINE HIGHWAY
May 1 to September 30, 1985.
Reprinted from a full rate schedule published by the ferry system.

Staterooms on the four major vessels, but not on *Aurora*, *Le Conte*, and *Chilkat*. All staterooms have shower, toilet and basin. Two berth cabins are hardest to reserve in peak season. Berths are upper with ladder, and lower.

	Seattle to Skagway	Prince Rupert to Skagway
Passenger, 12 years & older	$ 198.00	$ 91.00
Vehicle 15' to 19' long	607.00	269.00
Vehicle 25' to 28' long	1214.00	534.00
Motorcycle	194.00	87.00
Bicycle, kayak	Free	Free

Children under 6, free. Children 6 to 11, approximately ½.

	Seattle to Skagway	Prince Rupert to Skagway
Pet (free between Alaskan ports)	10.00	5.00
2 berth cabins, all ships	151.00	71.00
4 berth cabins, all ships	201.00	97.00
3 berth cabin, *Matanuska*, *Columbia* & *Malaspina*	172.00	80.00
4 berth with sitting room, *Columbia*, *Malaspina*	203.00	103.00

Dormitory room—rate per berth, all ships. Cabins assigned as needed. Occupants must be willing to share cabin.

	Seattle to Skagway	Prince Rupert to Skagway
	75.00	36.00

Matanuska, running between Prince Rupert and Skagway, also has 5 berth combinations, of 2 and 3 berth cabins.

For rates between other ports or for larger vehicles, see complete schedule. Meals are additional. Rates for passengers and vehicles are lower from October 1 through April 30, and the driver is included. No out-of-state personal checks are accepted. Payment must be made at least 45 days before sailing to hold reservations. Lower rates are in effect for all vehicles to 10' long (same as motorcycle rate), and for sub-compacts 10' to 15' long.

Reservations are strongly advised for cabins and vehicles. Cabin fares are paid separately for each segment if you plan stopovers. Walk-on passengers boarding in Seattle or sailing to Seattle need reservations.

Sawyer Glacier "calves" icebergs into Tracy Arm.

1985 SEASON

At press time almost all staterooms to and from Seattle are booked from June 1 through August. While there are usually some no-shows and it's worth signing the purser's wait list as early as possible, you can't count on it. In Seattle the purser's list is at the hut where the purser works at the head of the loading ramp. For all other ports it is at the purser's office aboard ship. As there is usually only one ship per week from Seattle, there will also be a shortage of room for walk-on passengers and vehicles to and from Seattle. Best chances for staterooms and car space are to and from Prince Rupert. Alternatives are traveling southbound during early summer, traveling earlier or later, or flying to one of the Southeastern Alaska ports and riding ferries around their route from there. From Prince Rupert the *Malaspina* and *Matanuska* have the most staterooms, the *Taku* has some, and the *Aurora* does not have any.

In 1985 the *Matanuska* is getting new engines and will be back on the run after leaving Seattle on June 17. Until then there will be no sailings from Prince Rupert on Wednesday and Saturday. Sailing times from Prince Rupert vary with tides to avoid having 2 ships using docks at the same time, particularly at Sitka. In port times at Wrangell and Petersburg have been lengthened, allowing time for a walk ashore on many sailings, though often at unlikely hours. Most Skagway times are from 1 to 3 hours though the *Taku* on Tuesdays and the *Malaspina* on Wednesdays are there for about 5 hours, making a good excursion from Juneau or Haines.

Sailings to and from Seattle

Columbia—Friday evenings, has 91 staterooms and room for 140 cars (though some of that is taken by freight vans). Sailings are at 9 p.m. Fridays. Reserved vehicles must check in before 4:30 or risk cancellation. Southbound Seattle arrivals are Friday mornings.

Sailings to and from Prince Rupert

Malaspina—Monday and Friday mornings, has 86 staterooms and room for 105 cars.

Matanuska—Wednesday and Saturday mornings, starting June 22, has 112 staterooms (mostly 2 and 3 berth) and room for 105 cars.

Taku—Thursday and Sunday mornings, has 44 staterooms and room for 90 cars.

Aurora—Tuesday mornings, has no staterooms but takes some cars. It goes as far as Petersburg and Kake.

Northern Panhandle

LeConte—has no staterooms, but takes cars and vans. Meets *Aurora* Wednesdays at Petersburg and continues to Skagway via Kake, Sitka, Angoon, Tenakee, Hoonah, Juneau, and Haines.

She goes to Pelican at least once a month all year, but more frequently in summer. In 1985 she goes in May twice, June three times, July four times, August twice, and September four times. For additional information, see the section on Pelican.

British Columbia Ferries
Between Port Hardy and Prince Rupert

In summer, British Columbia ferries sail between Port Hardy on northern Vancouver Island and Price Rupert. In winter they go as far south as Tsawwassen, near the city of Vancouver.

In summer 1985 the B.C. ferries are running all daylight cruises between Port Hardy and Prince Rupert, with all departures at 7:30 a.m. and all arrivals about 10:30 p.m., after a short stop at Bella Bella.

Schedule:	Lv Port Hardy	Lv Prince Rupert
June	odd days	even days
July	odd days	even days
August	even days	odd days
September	odd days	even days

The *Queen of The North* features food and drink service, day rooms for one-way travelers and staterooms which may be reserved for round trips, including four equipped for wheelchair passengers, and elevators.

1985 Summer fares, Port Hardy to Prince Rupert (lower in winter)

Passenger, 12 years & older	$ 50.00
Vehicle up to 6'8" high, 20' long	105.00
Vehicle over 6'8" high	157.50
Motorcycle	52.50
Staterooms, 2 and 4 berth	Prices vary with deck.

While the new dock adjacent to the one used by Alaska ferries in Prince Rupert allows ships of both lines to be docked at the same time, some of the arrivals and departures are presently scheduled so close to each other that it would be risky to plan to get from one ship to the other in less than an hour. You have to clear customs for the U.S. or Canada on entering, which takes time when a whole shipload of people is trying to do it. If the ship you are on is late due to tides or other causes, you would miss a reservation. In 1985 northbound passengers connecting with the Alaska ferries will need to spend at least a night in Prince Rupert, while southbound passengers not camping will need a night in Port Hardy. Except for some of the *Matanuska*'s Prince Rupert arrivals, scheduled for 5:30 a.m., most Alaska ferry passengers will not be able to connect the same day with the British Columbia ferry. **British Columbia Ferry Corporation, 1045 Howe Street, Vancouver, B.C., Canada V6Z 2A9.** Phones: Prince Rupert, (604) 624-9627, Port Hardy (604) 949-6722, Vancouver (604) 669-1211.

Sitka Run

On almost all ship arrivals in Sitka there is only one ship scheduled to use the dock which usually means a bus tour of town is possible, though some arrivals in 1985 are at 10 in the evening. In the past bus tours have been available for all arrivals at 5:00 a.m. or later (daylight until late September) with the museum open and coffee waiting! Sitka really does welcome you!

The four large ships are all scheduled to stop at Sitka during the early part of the week which makes an overnight stop easy. The smaller *LeConte* sails to Sitka several times a week, allowing you other ferry options.

Pair of loons on Turner Lake.

INFORMATION, RESERVATIONS

For reservations, schedules, and information: Alaska Marine Highway System, Pouch R, Juneau, Alaska 99811, (907) 465-3941. Long distance call from Alaska, 1-800-551-7185 and from all other states, 1-800-544-2251.

For information: Alaska Marine Highway System, Pier 48, Seattle, Washington 98104, (206) 623-1970, or call in Anchorage (907) 272-7116. A WATS toll-free line serves all travel agents west of the Mississippi.

TravAlaska Tours, 555 Fourth & Battery Bldg., Seattle, WA 98121, (206) 682-4101 and **Alaska World Travel,** 207 Main St., Ketchikan, AK 99901, (907) 225-6131 have computer terminals on the ferry reservation system. They sell package tours which include additional services. Sometimes they have ferry staterooms available in spring after the ferry system is booked up.

The *Malaspina.*

DRIVING THE ALASKA MARINE HIGHWAY—
YOUR WAY

The Marine Highway is a well-designed system with thoroughly competent, experienced crews, running along an incredibly beautiful route. If you simply get on at one end and ride to the other, you will have a memorable trip. If you want to experience more of Southeastern Alaska, here is how you can do it:

Getting to the Ferry

From outside of Southeastern Alaska, you can reach the ferries at the following locations.

SEATTLE (Pier 48)—Airline, rail, and highway connections. Airlines and Greyhound bus run between Seattle and Vancouver, B.C. The Amtrak station is about five blocks from Pier 48. Ferry sailings on Friday evenings.

PRINCE RUPERT, B.C.—Airline, rail, and highway connections from interior Canada; airline from Vancouver; and Canadian ferry from Port Hardy on Vancouver Island. Ferries sail almost every day in summer, less often in winter. In winter the ferry runs from Tsawwassen near Vancouver to Prince Rupert so one can choose whether or not to drive to Port Hardy.

From Tsawwassen, you can take the British Columbia ferry, with or without your car, to Nanaimo near Victoria. You can then drive up Vancouver Island or ride the bus (**Pacific Coach Lines**, 710 Douglas St., Victoria, B.C., Canada. Phone (604) 287-7151 to Port Hardy at the north end. It is a 6 hour bus ride. For additional information, **British Columbia Ferry Corporation**, 1045 Howe Street, Vancouver, B.C., Canada V6Z 2A9. Phones: Prince Rupert, (604) 624-9627, Port Hardy (604) 949-6722, Vancouver (604) 669-1211. Schedule and fares are given in 1985 season section. Rail information is in the Prince Rupert section.

HAINES, ALASKA—Haines Highway (connecting with the Alaska Highway) and bus service. (Alaska-Yukon Motor Coach.)

29

SKAGWAY, ALASKA—Highway, bus, rail connection to Whitehorse, Yukon. White Pass and Yukon Railroad stopped running their historic narrow gauge train over White Pass in October 1982 due to the closing of mines in the Yukon which had shipped ore to the coast at Skagway. The Klondike Highway connection to the Alaska Highway southeast of Whitehorse is scheduled to be open from May 15 to September 15.

Airlines—Most of the main ports in Southeastern Alaska have jet service with **Alaska Airlines. Western Airlines** serves Ketchikan (summer only) and Juneau from Seattle and Anchorage. Smaller air taxi services make connections to other towns.

For an enjoyable week, you could fly from Seattle to Ketchikan, and ride the ferry to Skagway and back in just over 2 days going direct both ways, or in 3 days if you go to Sitka on one leg. This would allow several days for stopovers in your choice of towns.

A Grumman Goose carries passengers between Haines and Juneau.

Stopovers at ports along the way are free. You buy a ticket to the farthest point you will reach and get a stopover pass from the ship's purser before you get off. Check the schedule when you are planning this to see which ferry you want to catch for the next leg. You may be able to make reservations (cabin or vehicle) before you leave the terminal if you have not done so already.

Walk-on passengers—It is easier to be flexible if you don't have a vehicle or a cabin, as there is usually space available on any of the ships for walk-on passengers. Get a reservation to or from Seattle, perhaps in Juneau and Haines during fair weekend in the third week of August, and between Juneau and Petersburg on the weekend nearest May 17, the Little Norway Festival. You may weigh this convenience against the use you could make of a camper ashore. In general, there are few roads to drive on out of town, and these are short. Drivers may spend time that they would prefer to spend sightseeing at ports in vehicle line-ups waiting to load or reload.

Vehicles—Leaving your vehicle in Seattle (see Seattle section) or Prince Rupert is one solution. Bringing a bicycle, free on the ferry, is another. Many people travel without vehicles, saving considerable cost on the ferry, and rent one as needed in ports where they stop over.

If you are traveling with a vehicle, you can plan stopovers ahead and reserve vehicle space for those segments of your trip. Once the cars are loaded on the car deck according to the ports where they will be unloaded, it is too late to change your mind. Note the required check-in times for vehicles at each port.

U.S. licensed vehicles may be left in Canada for as long as 45 days without a permit. In Prince Rupert they must be left in an authorized parking lot or with a private home where they can be parked off the street. They must be reported to the Inspector of Customs, either at his office in the Federal Building (Post Office at 2nd Avenue and 2nd street), to the right of the 2nd Ave. entrance or at the Alaska ferry office at the ferry dock before departure.

Recreational Vehicles—With increasing hotel rates, many people planning leisurely tours and stopovers bring camping vehicles or trailers. All campgrounds in Southeastern Alaska will accommodate vehicles up to 24' in length, with some having room for longer ones. Most spaces are not drive-through so you will have to maneuver. U.S. Forest Service and state campgrounds do not have hookups while most private trailer parks do. These are listed with the communities. Dump stations and sources for ice, propane and diesel are also listed.

During peak season, vehicle reservations to or from Seattle require early (January) applications and some luck. Reservations to or from Prince Rupert, B.C. are much easier to get. You can drive to Prince Rupert through interior Canada on paved roads, camping along the way, or ride the British Columbia ferry from Port Hardy at the north end of Vancouver Island.

The cost of carrying a vehicle on the ferry increases rapidly with length over 19 feet. Check the ferry schedule for details. The B.C. ferry has a surcharge for vehicles over 20' long or over 6' 8" high. There is a surcharge for vehicles over 8' wide on the Alaska ferry.

You will need to be able to back and maneuver the vehicle accurately. Seamen on the car deck will direct you, but you'll enjoy the trip more if you can do it easily. The length of overhang at the rear of the vehicle is important. While loading ramps are two stage and can be adjusted, the change from horizontal car deck to steep ramp at low tide is considerable. If you have more than a 2½' overhang behind your rear wheels, you may want to have a protective bar added there.

If you have a motion sensor or burglar alarm on the vehicle, you should deactivate it as the ship's motion may set it off.

You'll want to be sure your water and holding tanks seal tightly and check them regularly during the trip to be sure rough roads haven't started leaks. Propane tanks will be inspected and sealed before you board the ferry. Any spare fuel cans will be stored in the paint locker on the car deck after you board. Don't forget to pick them up when you leave.

Malaspina's crew practices rowing a lifeboat as part of the weekly emergency drill required by the U.S. Coast Guard.

If you fill your gas tank just before getting on the ferry, any increase in temperature may make it overflow onto the car deck, creating a fire hazard. To avoid delay, you should be sure your vehicle is in good enough condition to get on and off the ship unassisted. Be sure all switches are off before you leave it.

Remember that Coast Guard regulations will not allow you to stay in your vehicle on the car deck when the ship is underway and you will not be able to cook in it even when the ship is docked. You will be able to go to the vehicle whenever the ship is in port and at scheduled car deck calls when it is more than 8 hours between ports. If you run out of medicine, diapers, etc., and can't wait until the next port or car deck call to go to your vehicle, you can ask at the purser's counter for an escort. It's easier to plan ahead and bring what you'll need when you leave the vehicle.

On The Car Deck

A glance will tell you that the car deck is a working space, an equipment loading area. Eighteen wheel truck-van units maneuver in the small area along with cars, trailers, and RV's with blind spots from the driver's view. In summer when the crew is trying not to leave stand-bys behind at ports, you'll think they deserve a Golden Shoe Horn Award for fitting the last few in.

For your own safety and for the safety of the crew who may need the spot you're standing in to get out of a moving vehicle's way, these comments are offered. Passengers leaving the ship can go to the car deck as the vessel approaches the dock and the purser announces it. As the baggage car is often first off, that's your chance to put your gear on it for the ride up the ramp. Then you'll be ready to get off before the cars move. If vehicles are moving when you're walking on or off, it's important to follow the crew's directions to get across the car deck and stay on the walkway of the loading ramp without stopping unnecessarily. Farewells and picture-taking are best done on the upper decks. If you're standing by your vehicle to see if you have to get off, the safest way is to sit in it.

When you drive a car off, the crew and your fellow passengers will appreciate your not starting it until a crew member tells you to avoid unnecessary exhaust fumes on the car deck. If you will need help loading or unloading, you should ask the purser.

Staterooms—Staterooms are paid for separately from passage tickets. You can buy a passage and vehicle ticket for the whole distance that you will travel and then reserve cabin space, if it is available, for those segments on which you will need it. Four-berth cabins are generally easier to reserve than two-berth. Four-berth rooms have two lower and two upper bunks. Solo travelers may be able to use a single bunk in a room with others. The *Matanuska* has more two-berth cabins than the other ships. See deck diagrams at the back of this book for cabin layouts.

For passengers on a hurried trip, these offer a welcome rest. All cabins on the *Malaspina, Matanuska, Taku,* and *Columbia* have washbasin, shower, and toilet. All electric current is standard household. There is a closet and a ladder for reaching the upper bunk. Rooms are cleaned and made up before you enter, but cannot be remade daily by the stewards. You may request extra blankets and towel changes at the purser's counter.

Remember the alternatives to cabins: the recliner and forward lounges, and sleeping bags in the solariums. A suggestion based on personal experience: being able to stretch out full length is more comfortable for a whole night than recliner chairs which don't recline very far. With a foam pad or air mattress and sleeping bag, sleeping on the deck, inside or out (if it's not raining or you're in the solarium) is comfortable. Except for the Seattle-to-Ketchikan run, the time between adjacent ports is 10 hours or less.

Baggage: A powered baggage cart will haul your baggage between the car deck and the terminal on shore. You are responsible for all other handling of it. If you are riding beyond the next port, you should remove your baggage from the cart on the ship, for its safety at port stops and to leave space for others. While there is no limit on the amount of baggage you can bring in a vehicle, the baggage cart is for hand luggage only—not for freight, household moving, boats or rafts (even disassembled). Clearly anyone who can paddle a boat or raft is more able to pack it onto the ship by hand than the arthritic oldster who has to carry his suitcase because the baggage cart is full. The crew will show you where to put canoes or kayaks safely. I recommend you pack only the amount you can easily carry at one time. You don't need many extra clothes—Alaska living is simple. But don't forget raingear.

Binoculars are helpful for close-up looks at eagles and other wildlife. These, and anything else you will need en route, including medicines, cameras and film, should be brought to the upper decks before the ship leaves the dock.

Children: As on any long trip, people traveling with children on the ferry should plan for their interests and safety. The trip can seem long for them, especially between Seattle and Ketchikan where there is a day when the ship doesn't stop. There is no place on the ship to run that is not on someone else's ceiling. Quiet on the cabin deck is important to fellow passengers who may be trying to rest. The Forest Service naturalist may have some children's programs planned north of Prince Rupert. Walking ashore at stops helps. Games, books, coloring materials, sewing, knitting, according to age and interests would be worth bringing. One of those big doodle posters should last the whole trip. Older children might enjoy being provided with a simple camera and film to make the trip really "theirs." Climbing on the ship's rail is **dangerous** as the water is very cold and a child might fall overboard without being seen. For their safety you should know where your children are all the time they are aboard. Some children become increasingly nervous and active if they are allowed sweets during longer trips. They can find the trip a real adventure if you explore the ship and scenery with them as well as providing other diversions.

A play area for children has been added to the aft lounge of the *Taku* on the cabin deck.

Skagway's new ferry dock and terminal have a covered passenger walkway. Behind the vehicles in the background a new city-owned RV campground.

Seniors

During the off season, October 1 through May 15, senior citizens can travel free on a standby basis between Alaskan ports. This does not include meals, cabin, or vehicle. A **trip pass** must be obtained in person at an Alaskan port by showing proof of age (driver's license, Medicare card, or birth certificate). From outside the state the vehicle space and cabin can be reserved for the entire trip, e.g. Seattle to Haines, while the passenger fare would be paid to Ketchikan and trip pass obtained there.

Throughout Southeast Alaska many admission fares and some campground fees are reduced. Seniors can ride free on Juneau's city buses by showing a Medicare card. For reductions at Forest Service campgrounds you need a Golden Age card.

Alaska Airlines has senior citizens' fares 25% off regular fares.

Western Airlines has senior citizen fares on many of its routes, some with free stopovers. You'll have to inquire about the particular route.

The following information applies to **both** senior citizens and handicapped individuals of any age. The free passage between Alaska ports on a stand-by basis has been extended to **all year** on the **smaller** ships only, the *LeConte, Aurora, Chilkat, Bartlett,* and *Tustamena.* Note that the first four of these don't have elevators or staterooms. I don't recommend trying to travel on a pass on the Prince William Sound trips in summer or the *Tustamena*'s runs out the Chain. These runs are usually full and you could get left behind. You definitely should have reservations for these trips.

Passengers traveling on either type of pass are not allowed to reserve staterooms or vehicle space ahead of time. You can sign up on the stateroom waiting list with the purser when you get on the ship. However, if you're traveling with a vehicle during the off season, the driver **is** included with the vehicle. Since he/she is not then on a pass, that person can reserve vehicle space and stateroom (not free) for everyone in the vehicle.

Handicapped

People of any age who are so physically handicapped as to interfere with basic living activities, including working, may apply to the ferry system for a pass enabling them to travel free between Alaska ports from October 1 to May 15. This covers basic passenger fare but not stateroom, vehicle or food. The ferry system furnishes an application form which requires a physician's statement. The completed form is reviewed by the ferry system to see if it complies with the resolution passed by the Alaska legislature, and if so, a pass is issued. One should allow a month for this though the process generally takes less time.

Facilities for the handicapped are being added as the ships are renovated. Presently the *Taku* is the most completely equipped, with paraplegic staterooms, a restroom built for wheelchair use, and a ramp into the forward observation lounge. All four mainliners have elevators. On the other ships the crew will assist those who need help to the upper decks. Anyone who needs one of the two paraplegic staterooms on the *Taku* should specifically request it when making reservations.

Special diets are not provided on board though they can be heated in the microwaves on all vessels if you bring them. The stewards will refrigerate insulin if you request it.

Pets

Pets must remain on the car deck in vehicles or in strong containers, which must be provided by the owners. There is a surcharge of $5 for taking pets between Prince Rupert and any Alaskan port, and $10 between Seattle and Alaska. At stops you may walk your pets ashore. Most times between ports are less than 8 hours, but Seattle to Ketchikan can take over 39 hours and Petersburg to Sitka about 10 hours. Scheduled car deck calls will allow you to walk your pet on the car deck. Passengers are responsible for clean up and a scooper is recommended. Tranquillizers may be advisable for nervous pets for their comfort and to avoid barking, which carries widely through the ship.

Dogs really appreciate being walked at every port no matter what the hour.

Riding the ferry can be great fun for you, but probably isn't enjoyable for animals. In World War II we were supposed to ask ourselves "Is this trip necessary?" to save gas. You might well ask yourself the same for the pet. If he must travel, plan for his comfort with adequate space, water, ventilation, and his usual food. Even if he doesn't really need to go ashore, he'd certainly appreciate a pat and some encouragement at every car deck call or port—and you'll have a chance to spot any problem early. For its own safety, a pet should be leashed any time it's out on the car deck or ramp. If you have a bird in a cage, ask the purser for instructions.

Tugs maneuver a log raft through the narrows.

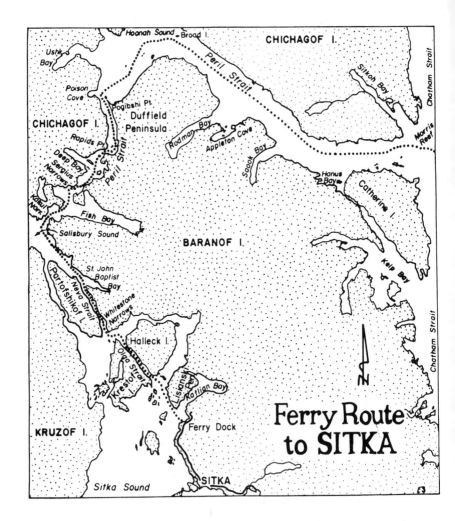

Sitka Run

Each of the larger ships, northbound or southbound, goes to Sitka once a week. The *LeConte* also sails there. It costs no more to go the extra distance when you are riding between Petersburg and Juneau, but it does take almost a day longer. The time will be well spent even if you don't stop off in Sitka, because of the narrow passages, great scenery and wildlife. To be sure of being on that run, check the schedule. The ship passes through Peril Strait, Sergius Narrows (where you can almost pick branches from the trees as you go by), and Olga and Neva straits. Leaving

Sitka you follow the same route back out to Chatham Strait. Since the ship must wait 6 hours for slack tide at Sergius Narrows, you may have as much as 3 hours to spend in Sitka. The dock is 7 miles from town, but there is usually time for an optional bus tour or a trip downtown if it is daytime and there are no other ferries using the dock. When the captain schedules departure time, the purser will announce if a bus tour is possible.

The bus tour passes all of the Russian buildings in town, and stops at Sitka National Historic Park and the Sheldon Jackson Museum (good Russian and Indian artifacts). A longer tour is given for people staying in Sitka.

To be sure of seeing the town, and of having more time to enjoy the museums and Russian buildings, you may want to stop over. Note that both the tour bus and the bus to town leave very shortly after docking, so board the buses quickly or you'll miss them.

Ships on the Sitka run use Juneau's Auke Bay terminal instead of the downtown terminal, avoiding miles of extra sailing and backtracking around Douglas Island. The Auke Bay dock is 14 miles north of downtown Juneau, and you cannot see the town from it. There is limousine (Capital Connexion van) and taxi service to town and to the airport when the larger ferries dock. The hourly city bus runs between DeHart's store, 1 mile toward town from the dock, and town from 6:45 a.m. to 1:00 a.m. Mon.-Sat. At presstime Juneau was offering a contract to private bus services for a bus to meet all ferries. In summer 1985 all ferries will dock at Auke Bay.

In daylight you have a fine view of the Mendenhall Glacier as you enter and leave Auke Bay. Unfortunately, many of the landings are scheduled at night, so if you want to see Juneau, you should stop over. Sometimes there's a tour bus to the glacier or into town during longer daylight stops, such as the *Columbia*'s southbound on Monday evening. Sharing a taxi for a trip to the glacier or town is another option, but do keep track of time if you're continuing on the ship. The drive from downtown to Auke Bay is over a half hour one way. Often the taxi must come from town to pick you up.

Smaller Ferries

You can see more of Southeastern Alaska by riding the *Le-Conte*, *Aurora*, and *Chilkat* ferries on their local routes. Based in Juneau, the *LeConte* serves the Tlingit villages of Hoonah, Angoon, and Kake, the fishing port of Pelican and Tenakee Springs on Chichagof Island, in addition to mainline ports.

Most passengers on these ships ride their marine bus regularly to shop in Juneau, Sitka, Petersburg, or Ketchikan. Some schedules allow them to come into town, shop for 4 or 5 hours, and return home. Before Christmas it's like being on Santa's sled without the reindeer!

In summer these ships are generally less crowded and have more relaxed, local atmosphere than the mainliners. If you have time and don't need a stateroom, the *LeConte*'s run from Juneau to Petersburg via Hoonah, Angoon, Sitka and Kake, will add another dimension to your trip.

Angoon is on Admiralty Island, at the mouth of Mitchell Bay, and at the west end of the Cross-Admiralty Canoe Route. Maps of this route are available from the Forest Service. Some of the portages have been planked and there are several Forest Service cabins that can be reserved for $10 a night (more details at the end of this section). The *LeConte* ferry service, takes you and your boat to Angoon and back without having to charter aircraft or larger boats.

Another interesting canoe trip that is now possible, thanks to the *LeConte*, goes from Hoonah to Tenakee, with only a short portage (shorter at high tide) between Port Frederick and Tenakee Inlet. The rails on this portage, making boat hauling easier, have been improved. For this trip you will want a tide table and some good judgment. Note that both of these canoe trips are on islands that have brown bears, and the portage is a bear trail.

Additional canoeing is possible from Pelican, but it is more awkward to get there and back, as ferry service is limited to one trip each month all year, more in summer. Charter aircraft do serve the area regularly. In 1985 the *LeConte* will go twice in

May, three times in June and July, twice in August and four times in September.

Kake is a good starting point for a trip to Craig (served by the Ketchikan-Hollis ferry) or a tour of the small offshore islands and coastlines of Kupreanof and Kuiu Islands. During waterfowl migration as well as summer, this would be a beautiful trip.

The *Aurora*, based in Ketchikan, goes to Hollis on Prince of Wales Island (connected by roads with Craig, Klawock, and some good fishing and hunting areas). The *Chilkat* goes three times daily to Metlakatla, which is a Tsimshian village on Annette Island. As the roads are flat, one of the best ways to see more of Annette is via bicycle.

The *LeConte* and *Aurora* have snack bars, and all 3 ferries can carry limited numbers of cars. Several of their trips make good 1- or 2-day outings, even if you are not staying over.

Sitting quietly near the beach and watching whatever comes by is rewarding in Southeast Alaska.

Photography

The Inside Passage is a great place for photography, whether you are professional or simply want a few nice shots to show friends back home. If this is your first trip here, the following suggestions, based on what works for me, may help. The frequent rain and fog plus the ship's vibration make planning worthwhile. On any trip you'll improve your odds for good pictures by being very familiar with the camera, including loading film and rewinding, before you leave home. It's also well to bring all the film you think you'll need, plus a bit more. Shops along the way may be out of the film you use. If your camera is electronic, bring at least one set of spare batteries.

For color I use Kodachrome 64 under almost all conditions. I usually use a skylight filter, sometimes a polaroid. Particularly in summer, daylight hours are long enough so you rarely have to shoot in twilight. For black and white photos inside the book I used Ilford HP-4, ASA 125, developed in Ilford Microphen. Most of the time I used a yellow filter, though some were shot with a polaroid filter. For bright days, especially along the British Columbia coast where there's a greater variety of trees, a green filter would be good for black and white film to make the forest look varied.

My cameras are two Pentax ME bodies (and a Pentax K-1000 for durable back-up), one with black and white and the other with color film. I use a Pentax 50 mm lens and a Vivitar Series I 70-210 macro zoom lens, switching them between the identical camera bodies,—and usually remembering to change the filters unless I'm using polaroid. The zoom is a marvel for photography from a ship where one can't control the distance to a boat or glacier. Unless you're going to use incredibly fast film, and shoot at very high speeds, 300 mm is probably as much as you can hold steady on a moving ship. I use a Tokina 28 mm wide angle lens for deck shots, sea to mountaintop scenery, and in towns ashore. The macro lens is fun to use for wildflowers on shore. I carry a changing bag for removing jammed film without losing the whole roll—rarely used but sometimes useful.

Keeping camera and film dry is all-important. Damp film jams easily in a camera. A rubber lens hood will keep raindrops off the lens or filter if it's not windy. In windy conditions with a telephoto lens, the hood may catch so much wind you have to remove it to hold the camera steady. I was able to keep working during an entire rainy afternoon in Petersburg by using a lens hood and tucking the camera in my rain parka whenever I wasn't shooting. I used a yellow filter to increase contrast. A good camera bag plus plastic bags helped.

On the ship, it's worth stepping out on deck for any picture you really want instead of shooting through windows. I dress warmly for the Narrows and stay out on deck (hypothermia in December!). The stern decks and several spots along the side decks on each ship are sheltered from the wind. From the stern you can photograph whatever comes up on either side, but there is more engine vibration. The side decks forward have far less vibration, important if you're using a telephoto. Photos used in this book were taken from both areas. Some spots on the stern decks have more vibration than others. I try not to let my camera or any part of my upper body touch the ship while shooting. Tripods are great on shore but pick up engine vibration you can't even feel.

Good luck with your pictures and the weather!

Exercise

For those who want to do more in fresh air than simply enjoy the scenery, you can work out brisk walking laps around the ships on deck, adding flights of outside ladders (stairs, to the non-sailor) where the open deck doesn't go all the way around. If you run on these, or play hacky-sack, it will be disturbing on someone's cabin or dining room ceiling—about 4 on the Richter scale. The lowest cabin deck stern on all the ships is above the car deck. Running in place here is OK. Jumping would probably bother the people in the nearest cabins. The deck rails are about the height of a ballet barre. With the ship's wake, luminous at night, rushing by, you won't even miss the music if you're doing stretching exercises at the rail or on deck.

For hard core runners, planning a long run the day before and after the ferry trip may help, especially on the Seattle-Ketchikan section where the ship doesn't stop. In Seattle, there is a long shoreline park north of Pier 70 where many people run. At port stops there is usually a road leading away from town for good running if time permits. You should be back aboard the ship at least 15 minutes before announced departure as the ramp goes up **before** the departure moment. Otherwise you may share the feeling I had once, hundreds of miles from home in a sweaty T-shirt and running shorts as the ship pulled out.

The turn around Green Rocks in Wrangell Narrows is tight.

The Narrows

The high points of any ferry trip are the narrows. Wrangell Narrows—the 21 miles just south of Petersburg—is a 46-turn slalom course for ships. In several places the channel is only 300 feet wide and 19 feet deep. Watching the precision and seamanship of your captain and crew is a thrill, night or day. At night the channel and range markers flash in red, green and white. Near Blind Slough, you can see 16 markers ahead, and it looks as though you are winding through a Christmas tree. In daylight,

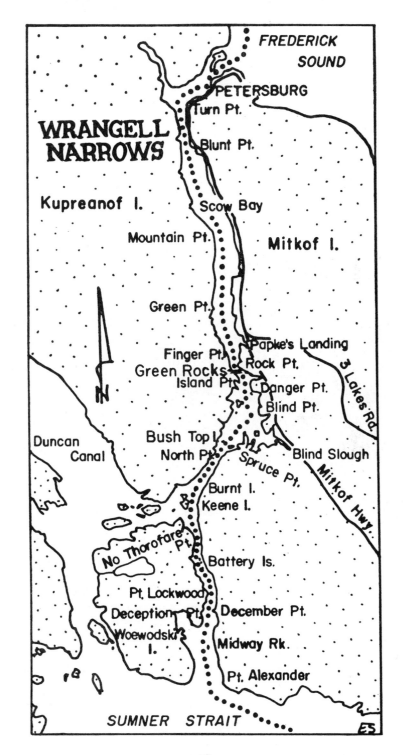

FREDERICK SOUND

WRANGELL NARROWS

PETERSBURG

Turn Pt.

Blunt Pt.

Kupreanof I.

Scow Bay

Mountain Pt.

Mitkof I.

Green Pt.

Papke's Landing

Finger Pt.

Rock Pt.

Green Rocks

Island Pt.

Danger Pt.

Blind Pt.

3 Lakes Rd.

Bush Top I.

North Pt.

Spruce Pt.

Blind Slough

Duncan Canal

Burnt I.

Keene I.

Mitkof Hwy.

No Thorofare Pt.

Battery Is.

Pt. Lockwood

Deception Pt.

December Pt.

Woewodski I.

Midway Rk.

Pt. Alexander

N

SUMNER STRAIT

ES

47

Wrangell Narrows and Sergius Narrows near Sitka, offer your best chances of seeing wildlife up close. These are eagle nesting areas where sometimes you'll also see deer or bears on the beach. Seals and sea lions haul out on some rocky islands. All of the larger cruise ships miss these channels, going around the islands instead.

A humpback whale breaches as *Matanuska* passes in Stephens Passage.

Whales

You may spot whales—especially humpback and killer whales —at any time. Sometimes the mate on watch announces them on the ship's speaker, though the mates are often shy about doing this because the whales sometimes dive soon after they are sighted. From the solarium, you may see whales come up behind the ship. Humpback whales tend to congregate in May and June near Juneau, Auke Bay, and the south end of Douglas Island. They can usually be seen July through September in Lower Stephens Passage, about 1½ hours north of Petersburg. Passengers traveling through these areas in daylight may see as many as 40 whales, often very close to the ship.

Bald Eagles

Southeastern Alaska has the largest remaining population of eagles—some 15,000 birds. The majority of them live along the coast most of the year. They nest beside the ferry route, and you can easily see them on their nests along the narrows in early summer. Between mid-July and September you will see some eagles, but fewer than at other times of the year, as they go up streams to follow spawning salmon. In fall and winter thousands of them feed on the Chilkat River flats beside Haines Highway, Mile 19.

Bears

Brown bears, the same species and irritability (caution!) as grizzly bears, live on Admiralty, Baranof, and Chichagof islands, as well as on the mainland. Black bears live on other islands, especially Prince of Wales, and on the mainland. You may see bears along the shore, particularly in the spring, near skunk cabbage patches. Fish streams and berry patches in season attract bears.

Fishing

The water you are sailing through supports one of the world's richest fisheries. Depending on the season you may see boats trolling, seining or gillnetting for any of the five kinds of salmon, tending crab or shrimp pots or lines for halibut or cod. When you are close to boats fishing, the ship's officers will often explain how the fishing gear works. Near the salmon fleet there will often be a large boat with a cargo boom and lights, the cannery tender, which picks up fish from the fishing boats and hauls the load back to the cannery so the boats can go on fishing. Some boats are equipped for more than one type of fishing so they can work more days a year. Most fishing "openings," or open seasons are regulated by the Alaska Dept. of Fish and Game. They decide how many fish must be allowed to spawn and set the times, often in hours, that fishing is allowed in an area. When the opening is only for 36 hours, the boats and crews fish all night!

In season you can sportfish for salmon, halibut, red snapper and Dolly Varden in salt water and trout and steelhead in creeks and lakes. There are charter boat operators and guides in every town. Often the sporting goods store personnel can tell you where there's a good spot you can fish from shore. Don't forget the fishing license, even for salt water.

The Greek-registered cruise ship Daphne docked at Skagway.

Cruise Ships

This booklet emphasizes the ferry system because to make the most of the ferry trip requires more planning and some knowledge on your part. During the summer many cruise ships travel through Southeastern Alaska. Compared to the ferry, they offer more comfort, more service, finer food, more shipboard entertainment, and longer stops at a few of the ports. If you want a considerable amount of personal service you may prefer a cruise ship with its huge staff of stewards providing for your comfort. Side trips may be part of the tour, or available as options. A day cruising in Glacier Bay or Tracy Arm is usually included. The small *Majestic Alaska Explorer* is the only cruise ship passing through the Narrows on its cruises between Ketchikan and Skagway. Routes and stops vary with the ships. Most offer rail, air or bus connections for tours including Anchorage and Fairbanks. Your travel agent can make arrangements for you. Most sail from Vancouver, B.C., but several start from Los Angeles or San Francisco.

The *Sundancer*, carries cars as well as passengers from Vancouver, B.C., through the Inside Passage, touring Misty Fiords and Tracy Arm, and stopping at Ketchikan, Juneau, and Haines. Drivers wishing to drive farther north could do so and catch a later voyage south. The ship will leave Vancouver on Fridays, arriving in Haines on Mondays. **Sundance Cruises**, Suite 1230, 520 Pike Street, Seattle, WA 98101. (206) 467-8200.

Shipboard Naturalist

Under an agreement between the U.S. Forest Service and the Alaska Marine Highway, there is a Forest Service naturalist aboard each of the larger ferries all summer, on trips north of Prince Rupert. You are traveling the length of the Tongass National Forest, which is the largest national forest in the United States. The naturalist provides a nature program aboard ship and sometimes ashore, answers your questions (or finds someone who can), and has a variety of handouts, maps, films, and a lending library. For children the naturalist has reading and coloring materials, a wildlife checklist, and sometimes special programs. All services are free. The programs vary with the weather, the facilities aboard the ships, your interests, and the different backgrounds of the naturalists. Programs are posted at the naturalist station in the forward lounge, and announced on the ship's speakers. During the off season the ship's purser often has a supply of Tongass National Forest maps showing the ferry route north of Prince Rupert.

Side Trips

Each town has charter planes and boat operators that can take you on scenic rides, and to out-of-the-way places such as Glacier Bay, Tracy Arm, the Juneau Icefields, the LeConte Glacier, and the Stikine River. They are listed under the ports from which they originate.

U.S. Forest Service cabin at West Turner Lake near Juneau.

U.S. Forest Service Cabins

If the Alaska you want to see has no roads or cars and makes few sounds but waves, wind in the trees, and waterfalls, you may find a stay in a Forest Service cabin a rare and exciting experience. For a bit of the wilderness all to yourself for a few days, this is it—with a dry roof! Some are near hot springs.

Most of the land (aside from the towns) between the Canadian border and Skagway is in the Tongass National Forest—17 million acres. Scattered throughout the forest there are 145 cabins that can be rented (by reservation) for $10 per night, for as long as a week, longer in winter. The cabins sleep between 4 and 8 people. Some are on the coast, and others are near freshwater lakes (these have a skiff and oars provided by the Territorial Sportsmen). Firewood, or an axe and maul, is provided. You must bring your own food, cooking utensils, stove oil if needed, sleeping bags, foam pads, life jackets, tide table, insect repellent, good rain gear and first aid kit. A small backpacking stove will

52

be useful if the cabin has a woodstove and green wood. The Forest Service will send you an equipment list if you ask.

For your comfort and safety on the charter flight you'll probably use to reach the cabin, and to avoid looking like a total cheechako, it's best not to expand on the list too much. Our pilot's comment "You people are awfully optimistic about the carrying capacity of a Beaver," as we crammed five passengers, besides the pilot, a German Shepherd, two fold boats, and a mountain of personal gear into the flying workhorse. However, I would add to the list two mousetraps. Baiting them with peanut butter, I caught 12 mice the first two nights at one cabin. If the cabin is in brown bear country (mainland or on Admiralty, Baranof, or Chichagof Islands), a heavy rifle or 12 gauge shotgun, if you know how to use it, is a good idea. To avoid bear trouble for yourselves and those who come after you, don't teach the bears that man is a source of food. Burn completely, or carry out with you **all** garbage and containers. If the bears are to survive and we are to use the wilderness, we must all do this.

You will be on your own, with no road or phone for help, once the pilot leaves you until the day he picks you up. If the weather gets bad, he might be a few days late. Plan your gear carefully, and **be careful** so no one gets hurt. Know how to avoid, and how to treat hypothermia. Wear lifejackets in the boat. Be extra careful with axes, fire, and while hiking. If no one stays at the cabin when you leave on day trips, it's wise to leave a note telling where you went and when you'll be back.

Some cabins are booked-up regularly, while others are rarely used. A few very popular cabins are reserved by lottery drawing from the reservation requests for certain dates. All cabins are shown and numbered on the Tongass National Forest map. The number indicates the office to which you should apply for reservations. Reservations are accepted no more than 6 months in advance. A table on the map lists the hunting and fishing available in each cabin's area. An Alaskan license is required, even for saltwater fishing. The table also shows how to get to the various cabins—by trail, boat, or floatplane. Charter operators in each town can take you to a cabin and pick you up. Generally, an hour's charter will cover both trips, though a few cabins are farther away. For reservations, apply to:

Sitka Ranger District	Chichagof and
Box 1866, Sitka, AK 99835	Baranof Islands

U.S. Forest Service Information Center — all other northern
101 Egan Drive — area, including Admiralty
Juneau, AK 99801 — Island and Yakutat

Petersburg Ranger District
Box 1328
Petersburg, AK 99833

Wrangell Ranger District   central area
Box 51
Wrangell, AK 99929

Forest Supervisor, Ketchikan Area   southern area
Federal Building, Ketchikan, AK 99901

These offices can send you a map of the forest, which is very helpful in planning your trip. It shows the entire Alaskan part of the ferry route. For a map and general information on the Tongass National Forest, you can also write: Visitor Information Service, Box 1628, Juneau, AK 99802.

For more detailed descriptions of what you can see and do in Southeastern Alaska, as well as several different viewpoints, you may want to read **Discover Southeast By Backpack and Paddle,** by Margaret Piggott; **Alaska,** by Norma Spring; **Milepost,** detailed annual; **Alaska Travel Guide,** an annual publication; **Alaska's Southeast** by Sarah Eppenbach.

Ferry Tale

A brown bear who lived on the portage trail south of Hoonah for many years was so big he was named "Boxcar." A man's hat wouldn't cover Boxcar's footprint and a six foot man holding his rifle at arm's length couldn't reach as high as Boxcar's territorial mark on a tree.

A monument near the hospital in Roosevelt Park commemorates the U.S. soldiers who left from here for the Aleutian battle of World War II.

Modern campground near the ferry dock in Prince Rupert.

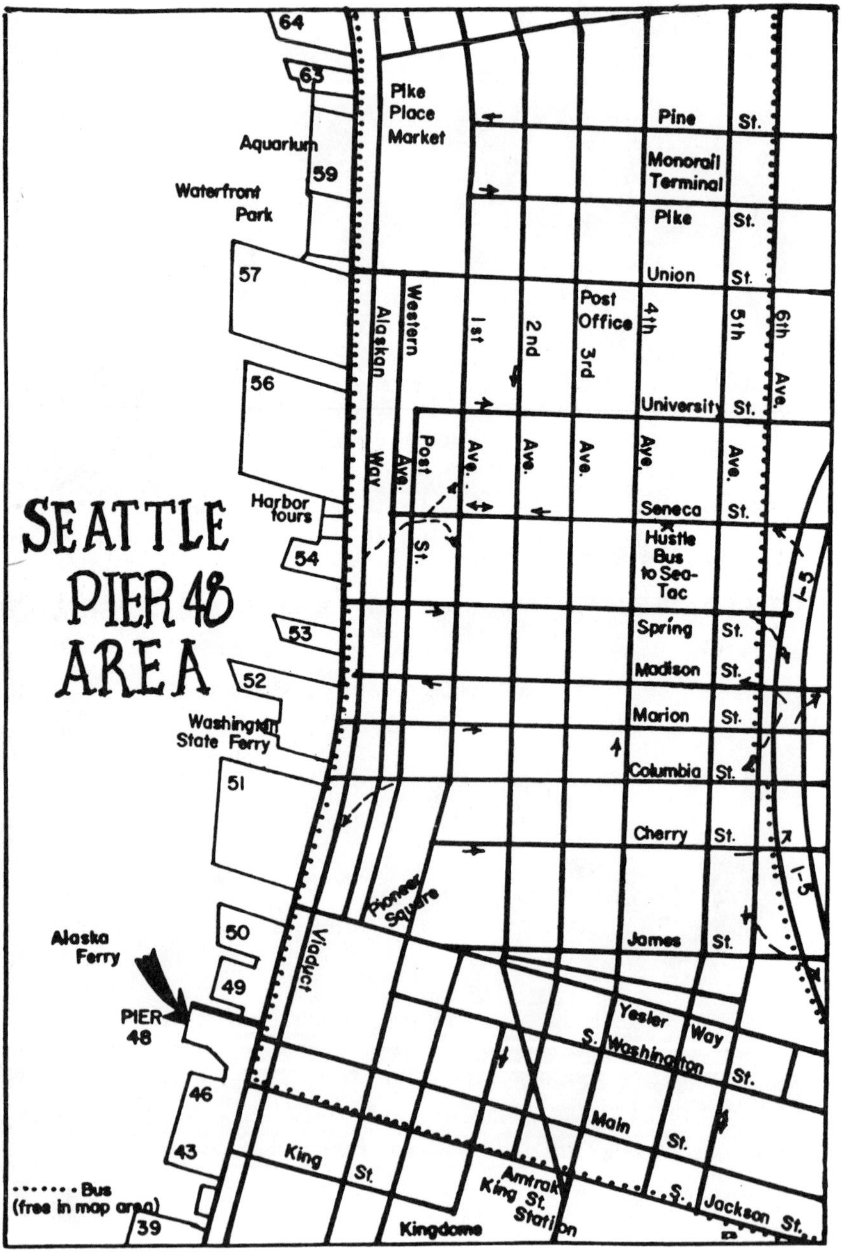

SEATTLE
PIER 48
AREA

64
63
Aquarium
Waterfront Park
59
57
56
Harbor Tours
54
53
52
Washington State Ferry
51
50
49
Alaska Ferry
PIER 48
46
43
39

Pike Place Market
Pine St.
Monorail Terminal
Pike St.
Union St.
Post Office
University St.
Seneca St.
Hustle Bus to Sea-Tac
Spring St.
Madison St.
Marion St.
Columbia St.
Cherry St.
James St.
Yesler Way
S. Washington St.
Main St.
King St.
Amtrak King St. Station
Kingdome
S. Jackson St.

Alaskan Way
Western
1st
2nd
3rd
4th
5th
6th Ave.
Post Ave.
Ave.
Ave.
Ave.
Ave.

Post St.
Pioneer Square
Viaduct

I-5

······ Bus (free in map area)

Pier 48 in Seattle, with the *Malaspina* on the right side loading for a trip to Alaska while the *Matanuska* and *Columbia*, on the south side, receive annual maintenance.

SEATTLE

SEATTLE is a fascinating city with a good public transit system and lots to see. Several guidebooks are available at Sea-Tac Airport and waterfront shops. Pier 48 is on the same waterfront where the Klondike gold-seekers once boarded ships for the Yukon. Nearby is Pioneer Square, part of Klondike National Historic Park (along with Downtown Skagway, and the Chilkoot and White Passes). Some of the original buildings remain standing, and many others are being restored. Art galleries, boutiques, restaurants and bookstores occupy many old buildings. You may want to stroll around the historic square, and share the excitement that the men of '98 felt as they packed to sail for the North.

GETTING TO PIER 48

FROM I-5, simply follow blue signs for ferries, directing you to both Alaska and Washington ferry terminals. The Madison Street interchange leads to the waterfront at Pier 52.

FROM SEA-TAC AIRPORT, the **Airporter**, airport limousine, takes you every 20 minutes to the Westin, Holiday Inn, Crowne Plaza, and Four Seasons Olympic hotels. From the latter you can walk about 10 blocks or take a taxi to Pier 48.

METRO TRANSIT (city bus) #174 runs regularly and cheaply between Sea-Tac and downtown.

RAIL—**Amtrak** station, 6 blocks, S. Jackson St. and 3rd Ave. S., on municipal bus route with line to Pier 48. Does not go to Vancouver.

BUS—**Greyhound**, 8th Avenue and Stewart; **Continental Trailways**, 6th Avenue, between Stewart and Virginia. Both are north and east of the area shown on this map. Greyhound goes to Vancouver and an affiliate continues to Prince Rupert.

TAXI—You can take any cab at a stand, not necessarily the first. Some serve certain areas of the city only. Since they have been deregulated, **Yellow**, 622-6500, and **Far West**, 622-1717, are the only ones which charge rates similar to the regulated fares. The others may charge as they choose. It's worth asking before getting in the cab.

LEAVING PIER 48

TO GET TO I-5 from Pier 48, drive off the vessel to the entrance of Pier 48. Directly in front of you is Main Street. Drive up Main Street to 4th Avenue, turn left on 4th, continue up 4th Avenue to Cherry Street, turn right on Cherry Street and follow the signs to I-5 North or South.

TO I-90 EAST: When leaving Pier 48, go straight ahead on Main Street to 2nd Avenue, take a right turn on 2nd Avenue and follow the signs.

TO SEE AND DO

Within walking distance of Pier 48 are:
• The Washington State ferry terminal for ferries to Bainbridge Island and Bremerton, Pier 53.
• Visit some of the 200 parks in Seattle and King County displaying public art purchased by the city.
• The Waterfront Trolley running 1.6 miles from Pier 48 to Pier 70 has three 1927 Australian streetcars very much like the ones which plied this area in early days. They run every 20 to 30 minutes from 8 a.m. to 11 p.m. in summer and 8 a.m. to 6 p.m. in winter. Some have singing drivers. All are wheelchair accessible. They are fun!
• Many waterfront gift shops, restaurants, crafts shops (including several on Pier 70).
• The Seattle Aquarium, Pier 59. Excellent. Open 9 a.m. daily to 9 p.m. in summer.
• Omnidome, 3D photodrama, Pier 59.
• Pike Place Market—across from the aquarium, with many shops on several levels. Open 7 days a week in summer.
• Waterfront parks next to the aquarium, fishing and shrimping.
• Several art galleries and bookstores.
• Seattle Harbor Tours, next to Pier 54.
• Cruises to Victoria, B.C. on the classic Princess Marguerite, Pier 69, April to October. Takes cars. (206) 623-5560.
• Cruise to Vancouver and Victoria B.C. on the Island Jetfoil. Pier 69, all year. Walk-ons only. (206) 623-FOIL.
• Kingdome Sports Arena, S. King St. and Occidental Ave. S. Tours 11 a.m., 1 p.m., 3 p.m.
• Chinatown. S. Main St. at 6th and 7th Avenues. Tours available.
• The Coast Guard museum, Pier 36.
• Klondike Gold Rush National Park, Seattle unit, 117 South Main Street. Free films and slide programs 9 a.m. to 5 p.m. daily, extended summer hours.

• The waterfront from S. Washington Street to Pier 67 is within the free zone for the bus system. The monorail, Pike and 4th, is a fast way to the Seattle Center, 1962 World's Fair site.

ANNUAL EVENTS

Seattle Seafair. City-wide marine festival: regattas, hydroplane races, parades, sports events, exhibits, etc. Late July–early August. Free.

Pacific Northwest Wagner Festival. Seattle Opera House. Presentation of Wagner's four-opera cycle, "The Ring of the Nibelung." Last week of July–first week of August.

Bumbershoot, Seattle Center. Outdoor/indoor festival of arts and music. Labor Day Weekend.

Folklife Festival, Seattle Center. Outdoor music and crafts. Memorial Day Weekend. Free.

Pacific Northwest Arts and Crafts Fair, Bellevue Square (four miles east in Bellevue). Art exhibits, handicrafts. Late July. Free.

ACCOMMODATIONS: There are several good guidebooks to Seattle available in bookstores and the Washington State ferry terminal. Downtown lodgings range from deluxe to the YMCA, YWCA and youth hostel. On the highways north, east and south of Seattle, and especially along Pacific Avenue near Sea-Tac Airport are moderate hotels, many from the national chains.

INFORMATION AVAILABLE: Seattle/King County Convention & Visitors' Bureau, 666 Stewart St., Seattle, WA 98101. (206) 447-4240. 8:30 a.m.–5:00 p.m., Monday–Friday.

For Washington State information, from out-of-state call 1-800-541-WASH; from in-state call 1-800-562-4570.

CAR STORAGE

Garages which will store vehicles while you ride the ferry include:

Apex Automotive Garage
410 Fifth Ave. South
(206) 623-8156

Office & Gate Hours: Mon–Fri 7 a.m.–6 p.m.; Sat 8 a.m.–12 p.m.
Rates: $2.50/day, $35/month, covered

Cherry Street Garage
213 Cherry Street
(206) 682-4520

Office & Gate Hours: Mon–Fri 7 a.m.–6:15 p.m.
Rates: $3.75/day, $40/month, covered
No campers

Grosvenor House Garage
505 Vine Street
(206) 623-0033

Office & Gate Hours: Mon–Sun 6:30 a.m.–1:00 a.m.
Rates: $2.75/day, $32.50/month, covered
Some motor homes and pickup campers permitted

Hal Thompson's Parking
2200 Alaskan Way

Hours: Seasonal parking facility; closed in winter
Rates: approx. cost between $3.00-$4.00/day
Note: 1½ blocks from Pier 69, Seattle-Victoria Ferry Terminal

Heliparking
1st Ave. & Union St.
(206) 623-0655

Office Hours: Mon–Fri 6:30 a.m.–6:30 p.m.; Sat 10 a.m.–5:30 p.m.
Gate Hours: Mon–Sun 24 hours
Rates: $2.40/day, $25/month
Note: 6'9" vehicle height limit

Marqueen Garage
10 Mercer Street
(206) 284-0590

Office & Gate Hours: Mon–Fri 7:30 a.m.–6 p.m.
Rates: $30 & up, depending on size, covered

Olympic Garage
5th Avenue & Seneca St.
(206) 624-5767

Office & Gate Hours: Mon–Sun 24 hours
Rates: $5/hour, covered

Seattle Parking & Storage
301 Madison Street
(206) 622-3717

Office & Gate Hours: Mon–Fri 6:30 a.m.–12 a.m.; Sat 8 a.m.–12 a.m.
Rates: $5.50/day, $62.13/month
Note: No trucks, campers or vans

Self Parking Garage
3rd Ave. & Stewart St.
(206) 344-7231

Office Hours: Mon–Sat 6 a.m.–10:30 p.m.; Sun 10 a.m.–6 p.m.
Rates: $4.50/day, $40/month
Note: Vehicle height limit 6'10"

Systems Garage
601 Olive Way
(206) 623-0925

Office & Gate Hours: Mon–Sun 24 hours
Rates: $1.00/hour, $3.50/day
Note: No campers, trucks, some vans

The rates quoted above may have increased since this list was compiled.

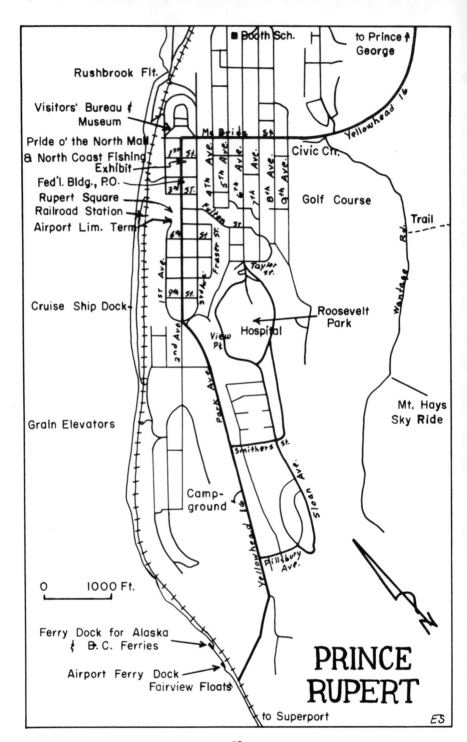

Booth Sch.

to Prince
George

Rushbrook Flt.

Visitors' Bureau &
Museum

Pride o' the North Mall
& North Coast Fishing
Exhibit

Fed'l. Bldg., P.O.

Rupert Square

Railroad Station

Airport Lim. Term

Cruise Ship Dock

Grain Elevators

McBride St.

Civic Ctr.

Yellowhead 16

Golf Course

Trail

1ST St.

3RD St.

4TH Ave.

5TH Ave.

6TH Ave.

7TH Ave.

8TH Ave.

9TH Ave.

Fulton St.

6TH St.

Fraser St.

Taylor St.

3RD Ave.

9TH St.

1ST Ave.

2ND Ave.

View Pt.

Hospital

Roosevelt
Park

Wantage Rd.

Mt. Hays
Sky Ride

Park Ave.

Smithers St.

Sloan Ave.

Yellowhead 16

Campground

Pillsbury Ave.

0   1000 Ft.

Ferry Dock for Alaska
& B. C. Ferries

Airport Ferry Dock
Fairview Floats

to Superport

PRINCE
RUPERT

ES

N

PRINCE RUPERT
(phone area code 604)

PRINCE RUPERT (pop. 20,000) is Canada's northernmost ice-free port. It is a lumbering and fishing center (mainly for halibut and salmon), and a transportation hub. Here the Yellowhead Highway and the Canadian Railroad from the interior meet passenger ships and freighters from all over the world. It is the main trading center for the Canadian coast north of Vancouver. The B.C. Ferry from Port Hardy and the Alaska Ferry arrive here several times a week. The B.C. Ferry has added ferry service to the Queen Charlotte Islands several times a week. It is worth taking time to explore Prince Rupert and enjoy the views over the harbor. Bald eagles dive beside the fishing boats, deer walk on the railroad tracks, and our captain once saw a black bear walk across someone's front porch while the ship was tied at the dock below. Atlin Fish Company has a cold storage room that is filled with frozen halibut (each over 100 pounds!) stacked like firewood. Lots to see here besides the fog.

TO SEE AND DO
See 25 totems standing throughout the town

• Enjoy the view of the harbor from Roosevelt Park.

• Visit the Museum of Northern British Columbia (Art Gallery and Visitors' Bureau in the same building). Open 9 a.m.–9 p.m., Mon.–Sat., 9 a.m.–5 p.m. Sun., mid-May through mid-September. Off season, 10 a.m.–5 p.m., closed Sunday. Donations. Two miles from ferry, McBride and First Avenue. 624-5637.

• Visit the Northcoast Fishing Exhibit. Lower level of the Pride O' the North Mall, Second Ave. Donations. Gift shop. 627-1102.

• Ride Mt. Hays Gondola. Three miles from ferry. Information: 624-2236.

• Explore the waterfront of this busy port.

• Take a city walking tour (maps available at Visitors' Bureau).

• Fish from boat, shore, or in the Skeena River—with B.C. license. Check fish and game or sporting goods stores to find out where and when the closures are.

• Watch reversible Butze Rapids from the highway, especially during tide changes.

• Ride harbor tours, with trips to Venn Passage and Metlakatla.

• Hike the trails on Mt. Hays.

• Enjoy the beautiful parks and gardens throughout the city.

• Pick wild berries in summer (get suggestions from Visitors' Bureau).

• Take a B.C. ferry side trip to the Queen Charlotte Islands with or without your car.

• Play golf on Prince Rupert's golf course or watch one of the summer tournaments. In this climate players often wear rubber boots. The course has an unusual hazard—ravens sometimes steal the balls!

• World War II historians or veterans of war in the Aleutians will find bunkers on shore, some visible from the ferry and some covered with undergrowth. Thousands of U.S. troops came by train to Prince Rupert and went from here to the Aleutians by ship. Several buildings near Seal Cove housed some of them. Roosevelt Park and a plaque near the hospital across from the park commemorate the action.

EARLY MORNING COFFEE SHOPS for those early arrivals! During fishing season, try the **Fairview Restaurant** on the fishing boat dock near the ferry dock. **Prince Rupert Hotel**, 2nd Avenue West & 6th Street. **Drifter Motor Hotel**, 1080 3rd Avenue West. All open at 6 a.m. Several others open at 6:30 a.m.

INFORMATION AVAILABLE at Prince Rupert Convention and Visitors' Bureau, First and McBride, 9 a.m.–9 p.m. Mon.–Sat., 9 a.m.–5 p.m. Sun., mid-May to mid-September. Off season 10 a.m.–5 p.m., closed Sunday. Very helpful people. 624-5637. P.O. Box 669ip, Prince Rupert, B.C. V8J 3S1 Canada.

If you haven't yet acquired a copy of the current Tourism British Columbia Accommodation Guide, this is a good place to get one; it lists hotels and useful info for almost every B.C. town and village. Free.

TRANSPORTATION

FERRY: **Alaska Marine Highway**, May, 3-5 ships/week; June, July, August, September, 7 ships/week. Winter, 2-3 ships/week. All larger ships have cabins. Drivers should look over terminal area in daylight, as the directional signs for vehicles are confusing. Alaska Ferry Office, Box 457, Prince Rupert, B.C. V8J 3R4 Canada. 624-1744.

B.C. Ferries run from Port Hardy at north end of Vancouver Island. Fewer sailings in winter when ferries run between Prince Rupert and Tsawwassen, suburb of Vancouver. Box 697, Prince Rupert, B.C. (604) 624-9627, 28, 29. Reservations: British Columbia Ferry Corporation, 818 Broughton St., Victoria, B.C. V8E 1E4 Canada. (604) 386-3431, or ZEnith 2020.

In summer 1985 the B.C. ferries are running all daylight cruises between Port Hardy and Prince Rupert, with all departures at 7:30 a.m. and all arrivals about 10:30 p.m., after a short stop at Bella Bella.

Schedule:	Lv Port Hardy	Lv Prince Rupert
June	odd days	even days
July	odd days	even days
August	even days	odd days
September	odd days	even days

To the Queen Charlotte Islands at Skidegate from June 2 to October 1, the *Queen of Prince Rupert* goes as follows: leaving Prince Rupert Sunday noon, Monday at 11 p.m., Wednesday noon, and Friday at 10 a.m. It leaves Skidegate Monday and Tuesday at 10 a.m., and Thursday and Friday at 11 p.m. Fare for a passenger over 12 years old is $12, for a standard car $45, and for a vehicle over 6'8" in height, $58.50. Note that all fares are in Canadian dollars.

The *Queen of the North*, a British Columbia ferry, heads for Port Hardy in early evening.

BUS: Meets ferries on arrival and departure. **Haida Coach Line** , 2nd Ave. W., 624-6236. Not meeting ferries, does provide twice daily service to Prince George, **Greyhound Bus Lines** (Canadian Coachways), 106 6th St., Prince Rupert, V8J 3L7, 624-5090, connects at Prince George to Vancouver. **Farwest Bus Lines**, 225 2nd Ave. West, Prince Rupert, V8J 1G5, 624-6400, local only, bus tours.

TAXI: **Skeena Taxi**, 624-2185, 624-2011, 624-2188. **Reliable Cabs**, 624-9666.

CAR RENTAL: **Budget**, 624-5144, and **Tilden**, 624-5318, 624-9470, are located in Rupert Square Shopping Mall, near the airport limousine terminal, 500-2nd Ave. West, Prince Rupert, B.C. V8J 3T6. **Kaien Chrysler**, 624-9645, 1250 Portage Road. Yellowhead Centre, 624-9645.

RAIL: **Via Rail**, Waterfront, at foot of 2nd St., Prince Rupert, 627-7588. Train service to Prince George several times weekly. Reservations office in Winnipeg is open Mon. 10:30–7:30, Tues. closed, Wed., Fri., Sun. open 7:30–4:30, Thurs. and Sat. 7:30–4:30. For reservations call toll free in British Columbia 112-800-665-8630 or see a travel agent, who has the other toll-free numbers. Amtrak has unfortunately stopped its run from Seattle to Vancouver. The 1985 schedule and fares between Prince Rupert and Prince George were being revised at presstime.

AIR: **CP Air**, to and from Vancouver, Rupert Square, 624-9181. 500 2nd Ave. West, Prince Rupert, V8J 3T6. Note: airport ferry to CP Airline flights leaves dock near Alaska and B.C. ferries, but passengers must check in at airport limousine terminal downtown (1st Avenue W., next to Rupert Square) and ride out to the ferry. Do allow time for this! Three flights daily in summer.

North Coast Airlines & Charters, Seal Cove. 627-1351. Serves Queen Charlotte Islands and other coastal communities.

Trans Provincial Airlines, Seal Cove. 627-1341. Also serves Queen Charlotte Islands and coastal communities. Scheduled flights three times a week to Ketchikan in summer.

Vancouver Island Helicopters, Seal Cove, 624-2792. No passenger service to Queen Charlotte Islands.

TOURS: Bus tours and service to interior points available from bus lines listed above.

A full list of tours available can be obtained at the Visitors' Bureau.

CAR AND BAGGAGE STORAGE

Car storage locations and rates (have run $2-4/day) were not set at press time. Call the Visitors' Bureau.

BAGGAGE STORAGE at B.C. Ferry Office (check for hours). Most hotels allow storage on day of departure for patrons.

SUGGESTION

For reasons possibly known to themselves, the U.S. and Canadian mails frequently take three weeks to get airmail between the U.S. and Prince Rupert. We advise using the telephone freely to make reservations or get information here.

Weathered pilings at Prince Rupert have character with grass.

HOTELS

Prices in Canadian dollars. Room tax is 6% to $49, 8% above that. Reservations advised in summer.

Aleeda Motel—900 3rd Avenue West, Prince Rupert, B.C., V8J 1MB. 627-1367. Quiet, clean, 31 rooms (some with kitchens), phone, TV. Single $30-38, Double $42-52, Twin $46-56. Add'l, $5/person, kitchen $5.

Commercial Hotel—901 1st Avenue West, Prince Rupert, V8J 1B4. 624-6142. 24 rooms (some with bath), restaurant, TV. Single $16, Double $18, without bath. Single $18, Double $18, with bath. Weekly rate, Single $60, Double $70, without bath. Add'l, $2/person.

Crest Motor Hotel—(1 mile from dock) 222 1st Avenue West, Prince Rupert. Mail: Box 277, Prince Rupert, V8J 3P6. 624-6771. Telex 047-89145. 100 rooms, restaurant, lounge, TV, wheelchair accessible, pets allowed. Fishing charters. Single $50-55, Double $55-60, Twin $63-70. Add'l $10.

Drifter Motel—1080 3rd Avenue West, Prince Rupert, V8J 1N1. 624-9161. 52 rooms, restaurant, lounge, TV. Single $36-44, Double $40-50, Twin $40-50. Add'l, $4/person. $5 cot.

Coast Highliner Inn—815 1st Avenue West, Prince Rupert, B.C., V8J 1B3. 624-9060. Telex 047-89212. Toll free number 1-800-663-1144. Restaurant, dining room, lounge, banquet facilities, wheelchair accessible, housekeeping rooms. Single $58, Double $65, Twin $65. Add'l $10. Kitchen $110.

Moby Dick Inn—935 2nd Avenue West, Prince Rupert, B.C. V8J 1H8. 624-6961. Sauna and whirlpool. Free parking, near B.C. and Alaska ferries. Single $40, Double $48. Add'l $8.

Neptune Motor Inn—1040 Saskatoon Ave. (Yellowhead Centre on Hwy. 16.) Mail: P.O. Box 966, Prince Rupert, B.C. V8J 3S2. 627-1377. Restaurant, cable TV, pets allowed. Kitchenettes. 45 units. Car and trailer storage. Single $34.95, Double and twin $39.95. Add'l $7. Kitchen $6.

Ocean View Hotel—950 1st Avenue West, Prince Rupert, V8J 1A9. 624-6259. 62 rooms (some with bath, TV). Single $20, Double $23 without bath. Single $30, Double $34, Triple $38, with bath.

Parkside Resort Motel—2 miles, 11th Avenue East and Hwy. 16, Prince Rupert, V8J 2W2. 624-9131. 33 rooms (7 with kitchen), phone, complimentary coffee, TV, pets allowed. Single $30-34, Double $36-40. Add'l, $6/person. Kitchen $4. Also has camper and trailer parking. 37 campsites, $9. Add'l adult $1, add'l child $1. Car storage $2/day.

Pioneer Rooms—167 3rd Avenue East, Prince Rupert, B.C. 624-2334. Boarding house. Single $15 ($50 weekly). Double $20 ($65 weekly). Twin $25 ($70 weekly).

Prince Rupert Hotel—2nd Avenue West & 6th Street. Mail: Box 338, Prince Rupert, V8J 3P9. 624-6711. Telex 047-8973. 95 rooms, harbor view, dining room, lounge, cabaret, wheelchair accessible, satellite TV. Single $42-46, Double $52-60, Twin $52-60. Add'l $10.

Prince Rupert Industrial Lodge—Yellowhead Centre, on Hwy. 16. 624-9727. Bunkhouse. Single $18 ($90 weekly). Double $22 ($110 weekly). Twin $24 ($120 weekly).

Rupert Motor Inn—1 mile, corner 1st Avenue West & 6th Street. Mail: Box 700, Prince Rupert, B.C. V8J 3P9. 624-9107. 51 rooms, restaurant, phone, satellite TV, sauna. Single $44, Double $52, Twin $58. Add'l $8/person.

Savoy Hotel—316 5th Street, Prince Rupert, V8J 3L5, 624-6751. 33 rooms (half with bath), phone, TV. Single $18, Double $25, without bath. Single $28, Double $35, with bath.

Slumber Lodge—1½ miles, 909 3rd Avenue West, Prince Rupert, V8J 1M9. 627-1711. Telex 047-8910. 77 rooms, restaurant, lounge, cable TV, sauna, wheelchair accessible. Single $42-47, Double $46-52, Twin $50-56. Children under 12 free. Add'l $5.

Totem Lodge Motel—¼ mile, 1335 Park Avenue, Prince Rupert, V8J 3R5. 624-6761. Mail: Box 518, Prince Rupert. 30 housekeeping units, phone, TV, limited car storage. Single $42-46, Double $48-52, Twin $52-56. Kitchen $5. Rollaway bed $6. Pets, $3.

No Youth Hostel. Note that there are inexpensive hotels in Prince Rupert.

CAMPGROUND

Park Ave. Campground—½ mile from ferry, 2000 Park Ave., Box 612, Prince Rupert, B.C. V8J 3R5. 624-5861. 100 sites, some pull-throughs, tent camping allowed. Showers, toilets, full hook-ups, dump station. $8.50 unserviced/tenting, $10.75 full hook-ups.

FACILITIES

LAUNDROMAT—**McBride Street Laundromat**, 326 McBride Street. 627-7755. Open until 9 p.m.

ICE—any gas station. **Northern Coop Store** across from campground. **Safeway.**

PROPANE—**Prince Rupert ESSO**, 250 2nd Ave. 624-3237. **Canadian Propane Ltd.**, 170 George Hills (near Cow Bay). **Northern Coop Store**, 1665 Park Ave.

DUMP STATIONS—**Campground** and **Northern Coop Store**, 1665 Park Ave., across from campground.

HOSPITAL—**Prince Rupert Regional**, Roosevelt Drive. 624-2171.

PETS—**Veterinary Services**, 975 Chamberlain, 627-1161. Boarding $3.50-5.50/day. **SPCA**, 2200 Seal Cove Circle. 624-2859. $4-6.50/day. Male cats must be neutered. Will take ferrets (not allowed into Alaska).

Camping trips by yacht are a popular way to enjoy the Inside Passage, enjoying good fishing and avoiding mud and bears.

BOATS

CHARTERS: For current information on boat charters, ask at Visitors Bureau.

PUBLIC FLOATS, FUEL. **Fairview public floats** just south of ferry dock. Fishing boat traffic is heavy here during summer. **Cow Bay Floats,** north of Atlin Fish Co., fuel. **Rushbrook public floats**, north of main part of town and fish canneries. Can be reached on land by going north on 3rd Avenue past Court House, taking second left. Launching ramp. Fuel at Cow Bay, adjacent.

HAPPENINGS

Year-round	Bingo, Wednesdays with Senior Citizens at the Civic Centre and Sundays at the Elks Lodge.
Year-round	Bowling, Friday evening and Saturday at Totem Lanes Bowling Centre, sponsored by the Senior Citizens Club.
Summer	Outdoor Archery, Tuesdays and Wednesdays at Seal Cove Field, sponsored by the Rainbow Archers.
Year-round	Crib Tournament, 3rd Tuesday each month, Senior Citizens.
Year-round	Art exhibitis change monthly at the Prince Rupert Museum Art Gallery.
June 6-9, 1985	Sea Fest. Parade, bed race, games, dance, concert, exhibits.

July 1   Canada Day Activities. Folk Festival.
A full list of things to see and do is available at the Visitors'
Bureau. Many not announced at press time.

CANADIAN CUSTOMS AND REGULATIONS

Vehicles can be left in Canada for up to 45 days without a
permit, under supervision in a lot, not on street. Report leaving
car to Customs, Room 105, Federal Building, or at Alaska ferry
terminal. When driving in Canada, especially the Yukon, carry
proof of adequate liability insurance. ($50,000/person; $10,000/
accident; $50,000/personal property.)

Note that there are several car storage areas in Port Hardy.

Carry money sufficient to pass through Canada by your
planned route and method of travel, allowing for emergencies, to
avoid being refused entry to Canada.

Personal identification is required for everyone, including in-
fants.

Firearms. Handguns are not permitted into Canada. Rifles and
shotguns for personal use are allowed. If they will be in B.C. for
a week or longer, you need a $1 permit, available from the
RCMP or Fish & Wildlife. Some sports stores may sell the
permits.

Pets (cats and dogs), over 3 years of age, must have proof of
rabies vaccination within past 36 months. Health certificate advised, within 30 days of trip.

Pilots. Canadian Customs now have 24-hour service, free of
charge, at Digby Island Airport, Prince Rupert. For others, including boats and floatplanes, customs inspection is free at Seal
Cove between 7 a.m. and 10 p.m. in summer. After hours, by
reservation made during above hours, the charge is $50. Winter
hours are 7 a.m.–4:30 p.m.

Boats. Pleasure craft have free clearance 7 a.m.–10 p.m. daily.
Overtime charges apply at other hours.

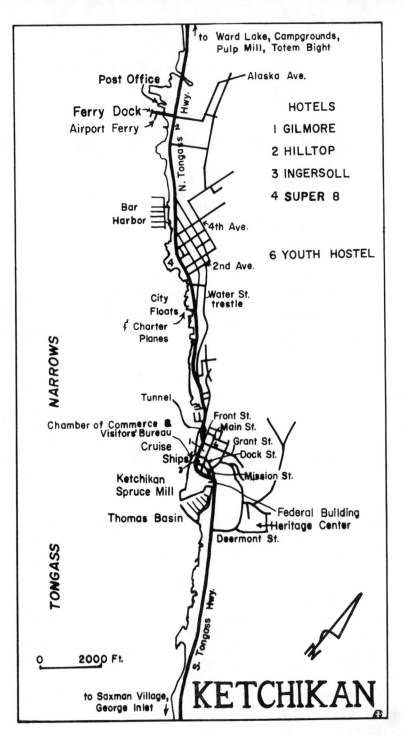

to Ward Lake, Campgrounds,
Pulp Mill, Totem Bight

Post Office

Alaska Ave.

Ferry Dock
Airport Ferry

HOTELS

1 GILMORE

2 HILLTOP

3 INGERSOLL

4 SUPER 8

N. Tongass Hwy.

Bar
Harbor

4th Ave.

2nd Ave.

6 YOUTH HOSTEL

City
Floats
Charter
Planes

Water St.
trestle

NARROWS

Tunnel

Chamber of Commerce &
Visitors Bureau

Front St.
Main St.
Grant St.
Dock St.

Cruise
Ships

Mission St.

Ketchikan
Spruce Mill

Thomas Basin

Federal Building
Heritage Center

Deermont St.

TONGASS

S. Tongass Hwy.

0   2000 Ft.

to Saxman Village,
George Inlet

KETCHIKAN

74

Creek Street was Ketchikan's red light district, with the houses now occupied by small shops and a museum.

KETCHIKAN
(area code 907, zip 99901)

KETCHIKAN (pop. 14,000) is the fourth largest city in Alaska, and the commercial center for most of Southeastern Alaska. Early Indians settled here. Later, salmon canneries and sawmills were built, and gold was discovered in the area. In 1954 the Ketchikan Pulp Company mill was constructed at Ward Cove, just north of town. From Ketchikan, planes and boats work in all directions, supplying logging camps, fishing resorts, and settlements on other islands.

The town, like most in Southeastern Alaska, is linear—never more than 10 blocks wide, but several miles long. Tongass, the main street, is built on pilings that take it out over the water in several places. Some of the cross "streets" are really wooden steps climbing the steep hillside.

The largest collection of totems anywhere in the world is found here at Totem Bight, 7½ miles north of the ferry dock. Saxman State Park, 4½ miles south of the ferry dock, and the

Totem Heritage Center, 601 Deermont Street, 4 miles south of the dock.

The ferry terminal is 2½ miles north of downtown Ketchikan.

TO SEE AND DO

• Take a walking tour of Ketchikan. Maps available at ferry terminal and visitor information building on downtown dock. Covers all the sights within walking distance of downtown.

• Take a taxi tour, including totem parks if you wish. **Alaska Cab** charters cabs for $36/hr. for 1-6 people.

• Visit totem parks. Saxman Village, 4.6 miles from ferry, Mile 2.3 S. Tongass Highway. Totem Bight, totems and ceremonial house, 7.6 miles, Mile 9.9 N. Tongass Highway.

• Totem Heritage Center, 4 miles, 601 Deermont St., 9 a.m.–6 p.m. Mon–Sat and 1–5 p.m. Sun, during tour season, June through September. Wed–Fri 1 p.m.–5 p.m. October through May. Fifty cents admission.

• See Deer Mountain fish hatchery with observation platforms and signs explaining the life cycle of salmon.

• See the Ketchikan Historical Museum, 2.4 miles, Dock St., adjacent to the library. Pioneer and Indian artifacts, minerals, shells.

• Tour Dolly's House, 2.4 miles, Creek St. This residence of Ketchikan's last "madame" has been opened as a museum, along with other Creek Street houses in this professional district. Open in summer. 9 a.m.–5 p.m. $2.

• Visit boat harbors and the waterfront. Nearest to ferry dock is Bar Harbor, about 1 mile, with most types of fishing and pleasure boats. Much of this can be seen during a regular ferry stop if you have at least an hour on shore—walk briskly, and keep track of the time. This is a good chance to see all types of fishing gear close-up, talk to fishermen, and see jellyfish and sea anemones under floats.

• Tour fishing harbor and fish processing plant (includes free samples). **Outdoor Alaska,** Box 7814, Ketchikan. (907) 225-6044 and (907) 247-8444.

• Ward Lake Recreation Area, 5.8 miles from ferry, turn off at Mile 6.8 N. Tongass Highway. Nature and hiking trails, picnic area, and campground. A good place to explore and learn about a temperate rain forest.

• See U.S. Forest Service Visitor Center on ground floor, Federal Building. Shows films, has historical and cultural displays and a variety of free handouts, maps and information. Takes cabin reservations. Open 8–5, Mon–Fri until late May. Open 8–5, Mon–Sat through first week in September.

• Hike trails to top of Deer Mountain (from Deermont) for spectacular view over town, waterways and islands. Perseverance and Talbot lakes, and White River. Maps available from Forest Service in Federal Building, or from information centers.

• Ride *Chilkat* and *Aurora* ferries on their local routes to Metlakatla and Hollis. *Chilkat*'s schedule allows you to go to Metlakatla for the day and return on her afternoon run. Hollis has no facilities, but offers road access to Craig, Klawock, Hydaburg, and Thorne Bay. Check with the ferry system about schedules.

• See Misty Fiords via daily tour boat from Ketchikan. Ketchikan visitors' Bureau has information at their building on the city dock. All air charter companies will make flightseeing excursions.

• Fish or kayak in Misty Fiords using Forest Service cabins or camping out. Kayak rentals $20/day, or bring your own. Transportation via air and M/V Misty Fiord on Sun., Wed., Fri. **Outdoor Alaska**, Box 7814, Ketchikan. (907) 225-6044, 247-8444.

• Fish from shore or boat. Mountain Point, 8.5 miles from ferry, is a favorite fishing spot for pink salmon, from mid-June on. Also has boat launching ramp and parking area. Residents can tell you the current hot spots. Fishing is *the* local sport here. Charter a boat, rent one, or bring your own. Do respect the tides, currents, weather and *very* cold water. Special 10-day nonresident license $15, all year $30.

• Pick berries in season—July, August, September for blueberries, red huckleberries, salmon berries. The big clearcut above the north end of town is a huge berry patch. It's less than half a mile straight up the hill from the ferry terminal.

Thomas Basin boat harbor in Ketchikan.

TRANSPORTATION

FERRY: Runs daily in summer; fewer sailings in winter. Dock and terminal are at Mile 2.3 N. Tongass Highway (north of town). Adjacent dock serves ferry *Chilkat*, as well as the ferry to Ketchikan Airport (across the Narrows on Gravina Island).

BUS: North end of the line is at the ferry parking lot. Buses run from here to the center of town, and south, every half hour 7:30 a.m.–10 p.m. Mon–Sat. $1.

TAXI: **Alaska Cab**, 225-2133. **Yellow Taxi**, 225-5555. **Sourdough-Ingersoll**, 225-6651.

CAR RENTAL: At airport, **Avis**, 225-4515, and **Hertz**, 225-5000. **Payless**, 225-4515. **National**, 225-6601, **Rent-A-Dent**, 225-5123, 2842 Tongass, and at airport.

TOURS—around Ketchikan and to totem parks, Ward Lake, etc. **Alaska Sightseeing**, c/o Ingersoll Hotel, 303 Mission St., Ketchikan 99901. 225-2740. **Westours**, Box 5097, Ketchikan 99901. Has summer number, 225-5930.

AIR: **Alaska Airlines** has daily jet flights between Ketchikan Airport and Seattle, Anchorage, Juneau, Sitka, Wrangell, and Petersburg. **Western Airlines** flies daily between Seattle, Ketchikan, Juneau and Anchorage, in summer.

The airport is served twice hourly by 10-minute ferry from the dock adjoining the main ferry dock. Be sure to allow time for the airport ferry in making connections. It departs from Ketchikan at 15 and 45 minutes past each hour. The uphill walk from ferry to terminal is two to three blocks. The airport bus, for a higher charge, stops at hotels and delivers you to the terminal door. 225-2888.

AIR CHARTERS: **Tyee Airlines**, Box 8331, Ketchikan, AK 99901. (907) 225-9810. Scheduled service to Craig, Klawock, Hydaburg, Bell Island, and Yes Bay.

Ketchikan Air Service, Box 6900, Ketchikan 99901. (907) 225-6608.

Revilla Flying Service, 1427 Tongass Ave., Ketchikan 99901. (907) 225-4379.

Temsco Helicopters, Inc., Box 57, Ketchikan 99901. (907) 225-5141.

Westflight Aviation, 1719 N. Tongass. Mail: Box 6440, Ketchikan 99901. 225-9693.

These charter services are based along the waterfront, and their takeoffs and landings provide much of the action in the harbor. Some also have bases on the airport. All can fly you into fishing resorts, Forest Service cabins, and virtually any place in Southeastern Alaska.

INFORMATION AVAILABLE at Ketchikan Visitors' Bureau on the downtown dock. Very helpful people. 131 Front St., Ketchikan 99901. Phone 225-6166. Chamber of Commerce, Box 5957, Ketchikan 99901. Phone: 225-3184. Also check with Fish and Game and Forest Service offices downtown. The Forest Service has an information center in the lobby of the Federal Building.

BAGGAGE STORAGE available at hotels, for patrons, on day of departure (check with individual hotels).

HOTELS
(plus 8% room and sales tax)
* 1984 rates last reported.

Clover Pass Resort—13 miles from ferry, Mile 15, North Tongass. Box 7322, Ketchikan 99901. (907) 247-2234. Lodge, cabins, restaurant, lounge, marina, boat rentals and supplies, fishing information and charters. Boat moorage. Package tours for three to eight days include cabin, boat, motor, fuel, bait, rod and reel, breakfast, lunch, dinner, fish packing boxes, transportation to and from Ketchikan. Trailers and campers $15 for 2 people. Add'l, $1/person. Season runs from April 2 to October 1.*

George Inlet Lodge—15 miles from ferry, 12 miles S. Tongass, P.O. Box 5077, Ketchikan 99901. Phone (907) 225-6077. Fishing lodge in completely renovated Hidden Inlet cannery bunkhouse which was rafted 90 miles to present site on the shore of George Inlet. Restaurant and bar. Specialize in fishing package tours including boat and preparation of fish to take home. Restaurant open to public by reservation for Sunday brunch and dinners Thursday through Sunday. Dates open: May 1-Sept. 30. Single $60, Double $75. Courtesy transportation by arrangement.

Gilmore Hotel—2.2 miles from ferry (downtown), 326 Front St., Ketchikan 99901. (907) 225-9423. 42 rooms, redecorated, new beds and furniture, color TV, direct dial phones, restaurant and lounge in building. Single $36-53 ($5 per additional person), Twins, Doubles, 2 double beds. Pets allowed—$50 deposit.*

Hilltop Motel, Inc.—across the street from ferry dock, 3434 Tongass, Box 917, Ketchikan 99901. (907) 225-5166. 46 rooms, restaurant, lounge, TV. Single $52-58, Double $60, Two double beds $64. Child under 12, $3. Crib $3. Add'l $5/ person.*

Ingersoll Hotel—2.3 miles from ferry (downtown corner of Front and Mission), 303 Mission St., Ketchikan 99901. (907) 225-2124. 60 rooms. Single $50-55, Double $55-60. Newly remodeled Charley's Restaurant and lounge off the lobby.

Ketchikan Super 8 Motel—½ mile from ferry, 2151 Sealevel Drive. Mail: Box 8188, Ketchikan 99901. 225-9088. 81 rooms, opened in 1983. Pets with permission. Rooms from $51-88.

Ketchikan Bed & Breakfast—525 Front St., P.O. Box 7735, Ketchikan 99901. Phones (907) 225-3860, 9277. Books travelers into private homes, can arrange tours, fishing charters. Single $40, Double $45. Confirms reservations with $25 deposit.

Rain Forest Inn (formerly West End Dorms), 1 mile from ferry. 2311 Hemlock, Ketchikan 99901. (907) 225-9500. Eight rooms, some available on per bunk, dormitory basis. Coffee shop. Restaurants nearby. Clean. Open all year. $15 per person.

Youth Hostel—First Methodist Church, 400 Main, AYH, 225-3319. Register 7 p.m.–11 p.m., $4. Memorial Day to Labor Day.

FLY-IN RESORTS: Near Ketchikan, offer a variety of rustic to modern facilities, and excellent fishing. Included are **Yes Bay Lodge, Humpback Lake Chalet, Misty Fiords Resort, Unuk River Post, Bell Island Hot Spring, The Floating Fishing Lodge,** and **Waterfall Cannery.** On Prince of Wales Island (and described in that section) by ferry and bus as well as by plane are **Fireweed Lodge, Prince of Wales Lodge, Karta Inn, Haida Way Lodge,** and **Log Cabin Sports Rental.** Information available from air charter services, Chamber of Commerce, and Ketchikan Visitors' Bureau.

CAMPGROUNDS
(14 day limit)

Signal Creek—U.S. Forest Service, 5.2 miles from the ferry, Mile .7 on Ward Lake Road, on the shore of Ward Lake. 25 units. Firewood, toilets, water, tables. $5.

3 C's Campground—5.4 miles from ferry, Mile 1 on Ward Lake Road. Walk-in campground, water, firewood, grates, tables, toilets. 4 units. $5.

Last Chance Campground—7.2 miles from ferry, on Ward Lake Road. Opened as needed for overflow from other campgrounds. Firewood, water, tables, grates, toilets. 23 units. $5.

Settlers Cove—16 miles from ferry, Mile 18.2 North Tongass Highway. Adjacent parking, with overnight parking allowed. Picnic area, beach, fishing, swimming, firewood, tables, grates, toilets, water. No hookups. Super view. Good berry picking in August. 9 units, free.

Clover Pass—private campground, RV hookups, laundry, dump station, 12 miles from ferry, $15/night for 2 people. Add'l $1. P.O. Box 7322, Ketchikan 99901. (907) 247-2234.

LAUNDROMATS

Launder Center, 830 Water St., 225-4444. **Convenient Laundry**, 2515 Tongass, 225-6711. **Southend Laundromat**, 301 Stedman, 225-3959.

FACILITIES

SWIMMING POOL: Ketchikan High School. Scheduled open hours. Sauna. 225-2010.

HOSPITAL: 3100 Tongass, 225-5171.

DIESEL: **Westside Service**, Chevron, Tongass Ave.

PROPANE: **Harbor Union**, Tongass Ave.

DUMP STATION: **Westside Service**, Chevron, Tongass Ave.

ICE: All supermarkets.

PETS: Vets are **Dr. Vern R. Starks** and **Dr. Terry Hensley**, mile 3, North Tongass. Mail: Rt. 1, Box 863, Ketchikan 99901. 225-6051. Note that they are the only vets between Prince Rupert and Juneau or Sitka. Pet boarding and dog grooming: **Gail Oaksmith**, 225-6393, and **Debbie Turner**, 225-6786. Boarding: **Bev Ohlson**, 247-8331.

BOATS

Clover Pass Resort—Rentals, supplies, launching.

CHARTERS

Outdoor Alaska, P.O. Box 7814, Ketchikan 99901. (907) 247-8444. Fishing, sightseeing to Misty Fiords, river raft trips, canoe and kayak transportation trips. Licensed for 20 people.

Alaska Salmon Charters, P.O. Box 8215, Ketchikan 99901. (907) 225-6487. Fishing charters, boats from 48 to 53 feet.

Ketchikan Marine Charters, 3420 Baranof, Ketchikan 99901. (907) 225-3293. Boats from 32 to 65 feet. Association of boat owners.

Leisure Adventure Tours, 3436 Tongass Ave., Ketchikan 99901. (907) 225-6641. Mini cruises in Southeast aboard 40-passenger boat. Also handles bookings for fly-in resorts.

HAPPENINGS

Salmon Derby, Special Derby Days, Memorial Day weekend and following two weekends. Prizes and fish are big.

4th of July celebration is Ketchikan's big holiday, with parade followed by a logging show with contests at the ballpark. Fireworks over the channel at night, many other events.

Alaska Seafest celebrates Ketchikan's fishing industry with many activities and exhibits. August 14-18, 1985.

Blueberry festival in August with crafts show, basement and lower floor of state office building. August 10, 1985.

Festival of the North Classical Music Festival, November 14-17, 1985.

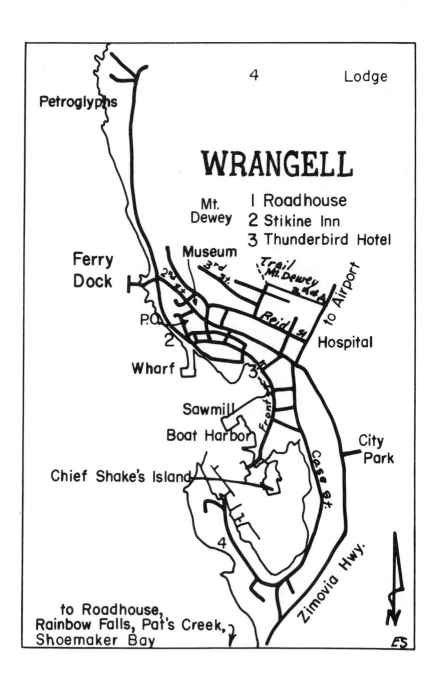

WRANGELL

1 Roadhouse
2 Stikine Inn
3 Thunderbird Hotel

Petroglyphs

4 Lodge

Mt. Dewey

Ferry Dock

Museum

Trail Mt. Dewey

to Airport

P.O.

Reid st.

2

Hospital

Wharf

Sawmill

Boat Harbor

Chief Shake's Island

City Park

4

Zimovia Hwy.

to Roadhouse, Rainbow Falls, Pat's Creek, Shoemaker Bay

N

Totemic painting adorns the wall inside the Tlingit ceremonial house on Chief Shakes Island.

WRANGELL
(area code 907, zip code 99929)

AT THE MOUTH of the Stikine River, Wrangell (pop. 3,000) is the only town in Southeastern Alaska to have flown 3 flags. The Russians built Fort St. Dionysius here in 1834 to guard the mouth of the Stikine against Hudson's Bay Company trappers hunting otters. Later, the British leased most of the area, calling their post Fort Stikine. Under the American flag, Wrangell, named for Russian Baron von Wrangell, became the jump-off point for gold miners headed up the Stikine to the Klondike and Cassiars. Today Wrangell is an important lumber exporting port.

Its attractions include excellent fishing, a totem park, a good museum, petroglyphs, and a variety of minerals, including the garnets sold by local children at the ferry dock.

TO SEE AND DO

• Visit Chief Shakes Island, one mile (a brisk 15-minute walk each way from ferry), in boat harbor just south of the lumber mill. In 1985 totem carvers may be working here and on Front Street. You will find a good collection of totems and a ceremonial house. Normally locked, it is open regular hours in summer, when tour ships are in, or on request in IRA Council office, 874-3505, or Wrangell Museum, 874-3770. Donations appreciated to help maintain the building.

• Tour the museum, two blocks up 2nd St. (the main street leading away from the ferry dock). Open 1–4 p.m. Mon–Sat., open for cruise ships and ferries on Sunday, in summer. Winter hours: Wednesday 2 p.m.–4 p.m. or by appointment. Wrangell Museum, P.O. Box 1050, Wrangell, 99929. 874-3770. Admission $1, children under 16 free.

• Take the Wrangell walking tour of sights, totems, etc. Map available at hotels and information centers.

• See petroglyphs carved by prehistoric Indians. The nearest is on the library lawn, next door to the museum. At least 20 more are carved in black argillite rock on the point about ½ mile north of the dock. From a sign on the road, walk down a boarded path to the beach. A few yards to your right you will see scattered black rocks with designs and faces carved on them. It is possible to make rubbings from them with paper and charcoal. Locals recommend laying rice paper on the petroglyphs and rubbing the paper with a wad of the bracken fern that grows along the boardwalk. These are prehistoric artifacts—please treat them with respect. Some may be 2,000 years old.

• Hike to Rainbow Falls. The .8 mile trail begins at Mile 4.7 Zimovia Highway.

• Fish in the harbor, or up Stikine River. Hunting also in Stikine Valley. Licenses and info at Angerman's Sport Shop, and Hesen's Hardware.

• Hike up Mt. Dewey for the view, 1 mile, trail starts at 2nd Ave. and Mission St.

• Charter a boat or fly up Stikine River for rockhounding (including garnets), river touring, and animal and bird watching (this is a major migratory flyway).

• Charter a plane to fly up over the LeConte Glacier and the mouth of the Stikine River.

• Meet local children (to whom the Garnet Ledge claim has been turned over) at the ship, and buy or just browse through the cartons of garnets they have gathered. Their salesmanship is often hilarious.

• Buy local garnets through the Boy Scouts at Wrangell Museum. Permits to collect your own are available for a nominal fee at the museum. Garnet Ledge is 7½ miles from Wrangell by boat or plane.

• Look at the small flattened pieces of dark-gray argillite behind the ferry terminal building. These are the same kind of stones used in Haida carvings.

• Watch totems being carved, duplicated and restored in 1985 under Wrangell Totem Project, which also includes restoration of Chief Shakes House. You can talk to the carvers and enjoy a close view of the ancient art at SNO Building on Front Street (yellow building on right side of street between Stikine Inn and City Market).

• The Wrangell stop is usually only ½ hour southbound, 1 hour northbound, but it can be longer depending on the tide in Wrangell Narrows. The Zimovia Highway (called 2nd St. at that point) starts at the ferry dock.

INFORMATION AVAILABLE at the museum, 2nd St., Wrangell Visitors Bureau, Box 1078-ES, Wrangell 99929. 874-3770.

Wrangell Chamber of Commerce office is in an A-frame next to the City Hall offices on Outer Drive, about two blocks from the city dock. Box 49, Wrangell 99929. 874-3901.

FACILITIES

ICE—supermarket.

DUMP STATION—Near Front St. and Case Ave.

HOSPITAL—**Wrangell General** on Bennett St. just north of Zimovia Hwy.

BOATS

No rentals known. Charters can be arranged to Garnet Ledge, Stikine River, and for fishing. Information on charter boat operators is available through Wrangell Visitors Bureau or at the Chamber of Commerce Information Center on Outer Drive.

Transient moorage available at boat harbors downtown and at Shoemaker Bay, south of town. Fuel, **Union** and **Chevron**, at waterfront.

HAPPENINGS

Tent City Winter Festival—celebrating gold rush in 1890's. First weekend in February. Fun, food, games.

Salmon Derby—Last 2 weeks of May. Dick Angerman, mgr. 874-3279.

Fourth of July festival—Logger's contests, Queen contest drawing for big prizes, food and games, boats, parade at 11 a.m. Midnight fireworks.

An eagle atop Wrangell totem lies down awaiting restoration.

HOTELS
(5% tax additional)

Hardings Old Sourdough Lodge—1 mile, Shustak Point south of town. Box 1062, Wrangell 99929. 874-3613. 21 rooms, laundry, TV, sauna/steam bath. Fishing and hunting trips. Pets allowed by prior arrangement. $65/person, double occupancy, including meals. Fishing tour package rates.

The Roadhouse—4 miles from ferry, Zimovia Highway, across from the new boat harbor at Shoemaker Bay, Box 1199, Wrangell 99929. 874-2335. Motel, courtesy car, restaurant, lounge. Salmon bakes, sightseeing tours, raft trips, fishing and hunting charters. Car and bicycle rentals. Pets allowed. Single $48, Double $54.

Stikine Inn—1 block on Front St., Box 990, Wrangell. 874-3388. 34 rooms with telephone, restaurant, lounge, dance band, liquor store, gift shop. Open all year. Single $55, Double $60, Twin $68, Triple $72, Quad $80, Five people $90. Children under 12 free.

Thunderbird Hotel—6 blocks, 223 Front St., Box 110, Wrangell. 874-3322. Courtesy coffee, laundromat, TV. Coffee shop across the street. Open all year. Single $45, Double $52, Twin $59. Room/car package, $59.95.

CAMPGROUNDS
(free)

City Park— Mile 1.7 Zimovia Highway. New restrooms, flush toilets and sinks.

Shoemaker Bay—Mile 4 Zimovia Highway. Self-contained recreational vehicles may park here. Near new boat harbor. Tennis court, dump station, tent camp sites.

LAUNDROMAT

Thunderbird Hotel—5 blocks from ferry, on Front St. 12 washers, dryers.

TRANSPORTATION

FERRY: Runs daily in summer, fewer sailings in winter.

AIR: **Alaska Airlines** daily, year-round.

AIR CHARTER SERVICE: **Wrangell Air Service**, 874-2369. **Diamond Aviation**, 874-2319.

BUS: There is no scheduled bus service.

BUS TOURS: Bus tours are available from the owners of **The Roadhouse**, 874-2335, 874-2336. They also run shorter narrated tours when ships wait for tides. Salmon bakes on request.
C.E. Bradley's, Inc., 874-3611. Features 1½ hour tour. Ten people minimum.

BOAT TOURS: **Traylor Enterprises, Inc.**, Box 1381, Wrangell, 99929. 872-2027. Stikine River tours. **Jerry Elliott**, 65' boat, 3- to 9-day trips, 4-person minimum. 874-3030. **Doug Smith**, fishing, sightseeing. 874-3447. **Dan Roberts**, fishing, sightseeing, LeConte Glacier Tours. 874-3637. **Bob Gillen**, Stikine River, 874-3191.

TAXI: **Star Cab**, 874-3622, 874-3511.

CAR RENTAL: **National**, Greg McCormick, 874-3314 has 2 cars. Make reservations. **Rent-A-Dent**, Thunderbird Hotel, 874-3322.

BAGGAGE STORAGE at hotels, for patrons, on day of departure.

Ferry Tale

A traveler standing in the *Malaspina* solarium looked up ahead and announced to his girl "There's another glacier coming up."
Without rising, she asked "Is it just your basic glacier?"

Purse seiners crowd into a prime fishing spot near the Sitka ferry dock.

Power troller, with poles but no nets.

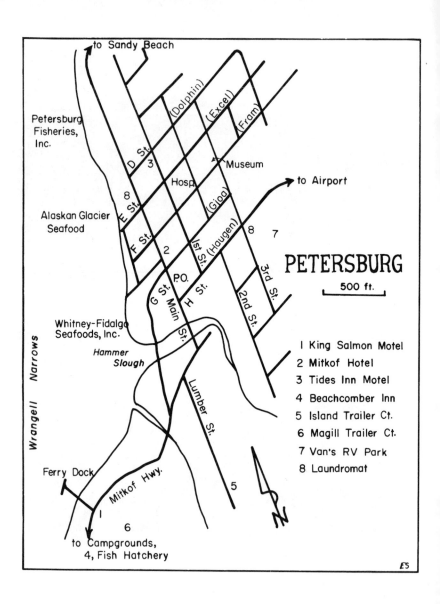

to Sandy Beach

Petersburg
Fisheries,
Inc.

(Dolphin)

(Excel)

(Fram)

D St.
3

Museum

8
St.

Hosp.

(Gioa)

to Airport

Alaskan Glacier
Seafood

E St.

F St.

2

1st St. (Haugen)

8

7

PETERSBURG

500 ft.

G St.

P.O.

H St.

3rd St.

2nd St.

Whitney-Fidalgo
Seafoods, Inc.

Main St.

*Hammer
Slough*

Lumber St.

Wrangell Narrows

1 King Salmon Motel
2 Mitkof Hotel
3 Tides Inn Motel
4 Beachcomber Inn
5 Island Trailer Ct.
6 Magill Trailer Ct.
7 Van's RV Park
8 Laundromat

Ferry Dock

Mitkof Hwy.

1

5

N

6

to Campgrounds,
4, Fish Hatchery

E5

92

The Coast Guard cutter, *Cape Hatteras*, and buoy tender, *Elderberry*, docked at Petersburg.

PETERSBURG
(Area Code 907, Zip Code 99833)

PETERSBURG (pop. 3,197) received the name from its founder, Peter Buschmann who, with his wife and eight children, moved here in 1897. The similarity of the geography to his native Norway, the mountain peaks, the fiords, availability of good lumber for building, abundant ice from nearby LeConte Glacier, a good natural harbor and its position in the center of the world's richest fishing grounds made this an ideal site for his new home. Today it is the main fish processing port in Southeastern Alaska, with four canneries, a cold storage plant, and a fish meal plant that reduces scrap. In season they handle five kinds of salmon, crab, shrimp, halibut, and herring.

Many of the people in Petersburg are of Norwegian descent, and the town is proud of its ancestry. Its Norwegian character is evident in its houses, gardens, and boats. In May, on the weekend nearest May 17, Petersburg celebrates a "Little Norway" festival, with Viking boats and Norwegian dancing, lots of terrific food, and costumes.

NOTE: Petersburg is renaming its lettered streets with names of historic boats corresponding to the letters. (Dolphin for "D", Haugen for "H", etc.) The older lettered street signs and addresses may remain for a time.

TO SEE AND DO

• Visit the Museum, 1 mile, 2nd and Fram streets, open daily 1 p.m. to 4:30 p.m. in summer. It has a newly expanded section on fish and fishing, including the world-record king salmon (126½ pounds), Cape Decision Lighthouse lens, Norwegian costumes, and other historical items.

• Watch salmon at Falls Creek Fish Ladder, 10 miles, at Mile 10.8 Mitkof Highway. Allows spawning salmon to pass falls into good spawning waters above.

• Tour Crystal Lake Fish Hatchery, 16½ miles, Mile 17.5 Mitkof Highway. This modern hatchery raises both salmon and trout. Formal tours are not given, but employees will explain the operation. Fish are sent from here to much of Southeastern Alaska. Open 8 a.m.–4 p.m., weekdays.

• Take a self-guided tour of Falls Creek clearcuts. A brochure is available at the Forest Service office in Federal Building, Main Street and Haugen Drive. You can see different stages of regrowth, experimental thinning, and fertilizing plots. Also a good view of Wrangell Narrows. Berrypicking in season.

• Hike out to three lakes on Three Lakes Loop Road Trail, mostly a boardwalk, built recently by the Youth Conservation Corps. There's good berry picking in several areas.

• Fish in Scow Bay, Frederick Sound, and streams. If you fish in the Narrows, beware of tidal currents and the suction and force of ship wakes. Do not get in the way of ships and tugs.

• Watch wildlife. In the Narrows, along the Mitkof Highway, and on the logging roads you may see bald eagles (this is a nesting area), otters, porpoises, bear, deer, and porcupines. Eagles often fish beside the ferry dock and perch in trees near the waterfront in town.

• See the U.S. Forest Service's "B. Frank Heintzleman Nursery," located nine miles south of Petersburg on Mitkof Highway. The nursery includes six quonset-style greenhouses and has a capacity of about one million seedlings per year. Scheduled tours are not given but can be arranged by contacting the Forest Service at 772-3841. Open 8:00 a.m. to 4:30 p.m. weekdays.

• Blind Slough Recreation Area. 16.6 miles from ferry, Mile 17.5 Mitkof Highway. Swimming, picnic area, daytime use only.

• Hike to Raven's Roost on mountain behind town. Overnight shelter available by reservation from U.S. Forest Service in Federal Building. About 4 miles each way, starting out road to airport.

• See the LeConte Glacier by charter plane or boat.

• Mountaineering for experienced, well-equipped climbing teams. This is the jump-off point for Devil's Thumb and other major peaks on the mainland.

INFORMATION AVAILABLE at Chamber of Commerce and Visitor Center, Box 649, Petersburg 99833. At Harbormaster's Building, Harbor and Excel St. 772-3646. Also the Forest Service office in the Federal Building.

TRANSPORTATION

FERRY: Runs daily in summer, fewer sailings in winter. Dock is at the south edge of town, .9 miles from the Federal Building.

BUS & TAXI: **Petersburg Cab Company,** 772-3811.

CAR RENTAL: **Petersburg Cab Company,** 772-3811. P.O. Box 818, Petersburg 99833. Reservations advised. **Avis Car Rental,** Box 1048, Petersburg 99833, at Tides Inn. 772-4716.

TOURS: Boat tours to LeConte Glacier (sail among icebergs in the fiord). **Chamber of Commerce Office,** 772-3646.

Viking Travel Agency, Box 1410, Petersburg 99833. 772-3818, has a list of boats for tours, including fishing en route to the glacier. Day to day availability varies with seasonal fishing openings.

Bus Tours of Petersburg and fish ladder and fish hatchery by arrangement with **Petersburg Cab,** 772-3811, or **Viking Travel,** 772-3818.

AIR: **Alaska Airlines** has daily jet service, year-round.

CHARTERS: Charter service and flight to Kake: **Alaska Island Air, Inc.,** Box 508, Petersburg 99833. 772-3130.

Temsco Helicopter, Box 829, Petersburg, 772-4780.

BAGGAGE STORAGE by arrangement with hotels.

HOTELS
(5% city sales tax extra)
*1984 rates last reported

Beachcomber Inn—3.1 miles from ferry, built on the water out of a restored old cannery, looks across Wrangell Narrows. Private dock for boats, planes and fishing. Salmon and halibut fishing in season at lodge. Box 910, Petersburg 99833. 772-3888. Rooms, restaurant, lounge, TV, entertainment. Single $51, Double $57.*

Narrows Inn—Across Mitkof Highway from ferry dock, Box 869, Petersburg 99833. 772-3291. Lounge, restaurant, TV, entertainment. Single $45, Double $50, some with kitchenettes. Add'l, $5/person.

Mitkof Hotel—1 mile from ferry (downtown), Main St. between Fram and Gjoa Streets, Box 689, Petersburg, AK 99833. (907) 772-4281. Older style, comfortable, centrally located. 30 rooms with and without bath, phone, TV. Single $52, Double $55 with bath. "Sleeping rooms" with use of hall restrooms and showers, Single $39, Double $44. Very clean. Courtesy coffee and rolls.

Tides Inn Motel—1¼ miles from ferry, 1st St., corner of Dolphin St., Box 1048, Petersburg 99833. 772-4288. 46 rooms, queen-sized beds, conference room, courtesy refreshments, phone, color TV with movie channel. Single $58, Double $70. Kitchenette, Single $70, Double $80.

A pair of humpback whales feed together in Stephens Passage.

CAMPGROUNDS

Ohmer Creek Campground—21 miles from ferry, Mile 22 Mitkof Highway. Bring water or boil creek water. Free.

Sumner Strait Campground—26 miles from ferry, Mile 26.8 Mitkof Highway. Boat launching. Bring water. Free.

Tent City—3 miles from ferry, out Haugen Dr. past airport. 31 tent pads, 62 people maximum. Purpose is to house cannery workers. Not family oriented. Restrooms, sinks, fire pits, wood, picnic tables. No vehicles permitted. Daily $2.50, weekly $17.50/person. Weekly deposit in advance.

Van's RV Park—1.2 miles from ferry, Haugen at 4th St., P.O. Box 763, Petersburg 99833. (907) 772-4552, 4680. Full hookups for 12 vehicles up to 35' long. Laundry. Bathrooms and showers. $10.50/day.

LAUNDROMATS

Glacier Laundry & Dry Cleaning, on Main St., near the corner of Excel Street.

Van's RV Park, Haugen at 4th.

BOATS

RENTALS: John Murgas, **Tongass Marine,** Box 1315, Petersburg 99833. 772-3905.

CHARTERS: **Fish Alaska,** Box 316, Petersburg 99833. 772-4816. Specializing in fishing tours, guided fishing. Check with Chamber of Commerce Office for recent additions to charter boat listing.
Viking Travel Agency, Box 1435, Petersburg 99833. 772-3818, has list and can arrange charters.

HARBOR: Moorage available. See Harbormaster. Restrooms. Grids to handle boats up to 50 feet. Water and electricity. Harbormaster's office, Box 1047, Petersburg 99833. (907) 772-4688. Monitor Channel 16 VHF and CB Channel 9.
Petersburg Shipwrights, boat pull out and grid. 772-3596.

FACILITIES

PROPANE: **Skylark Welding,** Box 654, Petersburg, 99833. 772-3145.

DIESEL: Union Oil tanks on **Union Oil** dock. 772-4219.

DUMP STATION: **AK Chevron Gas Station,** one block north of ferry terminal. 772-3740.

ICE: **The Trading Union, Inc.** (general store).

HOSPITAL: 13 beds with limited medical capabilities. Three

doctors, six emergency medical technicians, city operated ambulance. Two dentists, 1st and Excel Streets. 772-4291.

HOT TUB AND SAUNA at **The Spa** in Mitkof Hotel building, Main Street.

HAPPENINGS

Little Norway festival on May 17–19, 1985, celebrating Norwegian Independence Day (May 17). Need reservation for rooms or a sleeping bag.

3rd Annual Jaycee's Salmon Derby, June 1985. Over $3,000 cash and prizes for largest salmon.

Fourth of July enthusiastically celebrated by visitors and residents. Logging competition, street games, fireworks display. Miss Petersburg contest.

The *Glacier Bay Explorer* refuels at Petersburg on its way south for the winter.

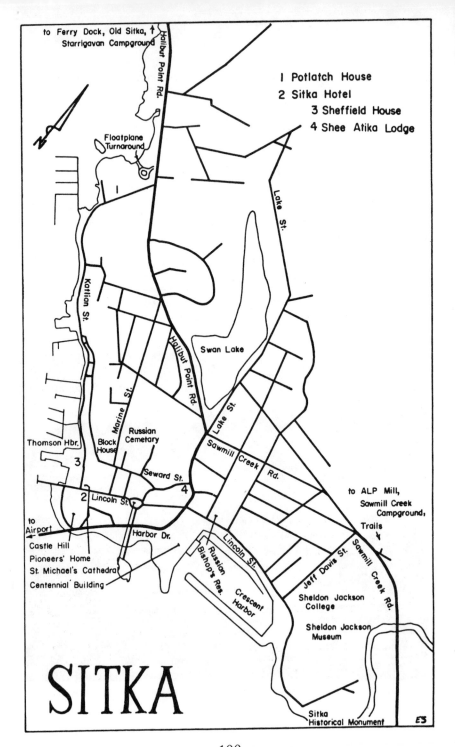

to Ferry Dock, Old Sitka,
Starrigavan Campground

1 Potlatch House
2 Sitka Hotel
3 Sheffield House
4 Shee Atika Lodge

Halibut Point Rd.

Floatplane
Turnaround

Lake St.

Katlian St.

Halibut Point Rd.

Swan Lake

Lake St.

Marine St.

Russian
Cemetary

Sawmill Creek Rd.

Thomson Hbr.

Block
House

3

Seward St.

4

to ALP Mill,
Sawmill Creek
Campground,
Trails

2 Lincoln St.

to
Airport

Harbor Dr.

Castle Hill
Pioneers' Home
St. Michael's Cathedral
Centennial Building

Lincoln St.

Russian
Bishop's Res.

Crescent
Harbor

Jeff Davis St.

Sawmill Creek Rd.

Sheldon Jackson
College

Sheldon Jackson
Museum

SITKA

Sitka
Historical Monument

ES

Tlingit canoe in front of Sitka's centennial building.

SITKA
(Area Code 907, Zip Code 99835)

SITKA (pop. 7,803) was the site of the first Russian Settlement in Southeast Alaska, established by Baranof in 1799. Originally located just north of where the ferry terminal now stands, it was wiped out by Tlingit Indians. A new fort and town were built at the present townsite. For several years Sitka was the European cultural center of the Pacific. It had the first shipyard and built the first steam-driven vessel in the Pacific. American, Spanish, and British ships came here to trade with the Russians for otter pelts. When the United States bought Alaska from the Russians in 1867, the change-over took place in Sitka. Her Russian heritage, her historic sites and buildings, the Sheldon Jackson Museum (with its excellent Indian collection), and the Sitka National Historical Park make a stopover here very rewarding. The Alaska Lumber Company's pulp mill, just south of town, provides much of the economic support for this area.

TO SEE AND DO
(Ferry dock is 7.1 miles north of town)

• Tour Sitka National Historical Park, about 9 miles from the ferry. See its program on Sitka's history and Tlingit culture. Visit workshops teaching Tlingit arts. This is the site of the Tlingit fort and "Battle of Sitka." Walk forest and beach paths with totems. Park is open 8 a.m. to 11 p.m. in summer. Picnic area.

• See the museum at Sheldon Jackson College, 8½ miles from ferry, 747-8981. It has a large collection of artifacts from all the Alaska native cultures. Recently acquired by the state, the building is being renovated. Opening planned May 15, 1985. Will be closed after Oct. 1, 1985 for restoration of exhibits. Summer hours: 8 a.m. to 5 p.m. daily. Donations appreciated.

• Visit the Centennial Building's wildlife and historical exhibits. Open 8 a.m. to 5 p.m., Mon.–Sat., May 15–October 1. 8 a.m. to 1 p.m. Sunday, June 2–Sept. 22 only. Winter, 8–5 Mon.–Fri., 10–4 Sat.

• Tour the Russian Bishop's House, still being restored. Open when cruise ships are in. Check with Sitka Nat'l. Historical Park, (907) 747-6281.

• See the New Archangel Dancers in a program of Russian folkdances at the Centennial Building (downtown). Check there for times of programs. $2 admission. Excellent performance.

• Tour St. Michael's Cathedral, 7.1 miles from ferry, at center of town. This is a Russian Orthodox cathedral, replica of the original which burned in 1966. The icons, doors, and other items were saved from the original. Open 11 a.m. to 3 p.m., Monday through Saturday. On cruise ship days 9 a.m.–3 p.m. Sunday 12 noon–3 p.m., in summer. By special appointment the rest of the year. Check with Father Eugene, 747-3340. Donation, $1.

• Walk or take a bus tour to Sitka's historical sites. These include: Castle Hill, Russian cemetery, blockhouse, Russian cannons, Russian Bishop's Residence, Pioneer's Home, Sitka Nat'l. Cemetary (veterans).

On the bus tour you will see the Sitka National Historical Park, Sheldon Jackson Museum, St. Michael's Cathedral, Old Sitka, Castle Hill, and the Russian Bishop's House. Some days admission to the New Archangel Dancers is included.

• Watch pink salmon and a few cohos migrate up Starrigavan Creek along road ½ mile north of ferry terminal, late July through September. Eagles usually in trees. Good walk for children.

• Hike local trails, including Mt. Verstovia (past Russian charcoal pits, and through 130-year-old clearcut) and Harbor Mt. trail (for an easily accessible look at alpine tundra, and a good view of the Sitka area). Remember this is brown bear country!

• Visit Old Sitka, ½ mile north of the ferry dock. This is the site of the first Russian settlement (1799), destroyed by the Tlingits (1802).

• Boat tour Sitka Sound. Special tours to bird refuge islands.

• Fly over Mt. Edgecumbe, Southeastern Alaska's only volcano (dormant except on April Fools' Day). You can reach the top by trail from the beach on Kruzof Island if you go by boat or plane.

• Fish from boat or shore. Inquire locally about hot spots.

INFORMATION AVAILABLE from the **Sitka Visitors Bureau**, Box 1226, Sitka 99835. 747-3940. Located in the Centennial Building.

The **U.S. Forest Service office** is in a new building on Katlian Street next to the Potlatch House, three blocks from the center of town. Forest Supervisor, Chatham Area, Box 1980, Sitka 99835. 747-6671.

Sitka National Historical Park, Box 738, Sitka, AK 99835, (907)747-6281, also has information. **Alaska State Division of Parks**, HPR Box 142, Sitka 99835. 747-6279.

TRANSPORTATION

FERRY: **Alaska Marine Highway.** Eight ships per week (both northbound and southbound) in summer; fewer in winter. Dock is 7.1 miles north of town.

BUS: **Sitka Bus Lines**, (907) 747-8443. Buses meet ferry for ride downtown. They leave very shortly after ship docks. $2.50 one way.

TAXI: **Island Cab**, 747-8657. 128 Lincoln. Box 4531, Mt. Edgecumbe. Inquire about rates. Car rental may be cheaper if you need more than two rides.

CAR RENTALS: **Avis**, 996-2404. **Budget**, 966-2250. Both in airport terminal.

TOURS: **Sitka Bus Lines**, 747-8443. The tour lasts 3 hours and costs $17.50 per adult, children 1/2 price. Morning and afternoon tours daily in summer with pick-ups at all four hotels. Ferry stopover tour is two hours, $8 adults, $4 child, when the ferry arrives at a reasonable (even 5 a.m.!) hour and will be in port long enough. Excellent guides.

BOAT TOURS: Silver Bay Cruise, M/V St. Michael and M/V St. Aquilina leave Crescent Harbor at 6 p.m., June 1–Sept. 1, Sat., Sun., Mon. **Allen Marine Tours**, Box 1049, Sitka 99835, (907) 747-8941. $20/adult, $10/child. Two-hour tour. Reservations advised.

AIR: **Alaska Airlines** has daily service to Seattle, Anchorage, Juneau, Ketchikan, Petersburg.

AIR CHARTERS: **Bell Air**, Box 371, Sitka 99835, (907) 747-8636. **Riggs Flying Service**, next to Sitka Airport. Box 883, Sitka 99835. 966-2444. **Mountain Aviation**, at Sitka Airport. Box 875, Sitka 99835. 747-6000.

BAGGAGE STORAGE in hotels, for patrons only, on day of departure.

HOTELS
(rates plus 4% tax)
*1984 rates

Potlatch House (motel)—5.5 miles from ferry at the end of Katlian St., Box 58, Sitka 99835, 747-8611. 30 units, dinner restaurant, lounge. Single $45, Double $55. View of harbor, Mt. Edgecumbe. No pets.*

Shee Atika Lodge—7.3 miles from ferry, 330 Seward St., Sitka 99835. 747-6241. 93 rooms, dining room, bar. Single $72, Double $82. Children under 17 free. No pets. 1-800-426-0670 for U.S. (including Alaska and Hawaii) and 1-800-552-7122 in Washington State.

Sheffield Sitka—7.1 miles from ferry, on waterfront, Box 318, Sitka 99835. 747-6616. 80 rooms, dining room, lounge, boat marina. Single $60, Double $72. Add'l, $6/person. Pets allowed.*

Sitka Hotel—7.1 miles from ferry, 118 Lincoln St., Box 679, Sitka 99835. 747-3288. 60 rooms. Single $36.30, Double $41.14. Single without bath $31.46. No pets. Larger rooms additional.

Youth Hostel—Methodist Church, 303 Kim Sham Street, Mail: Box 2645, Sitka 99835. 747-6332. Eight-minute walk from downtown. Open June 1–September 1. Check in 6 p.m.–10 p.m. Out by 8:00 a.m. No showers. $3.00 with AYH card, $5.00 without.

CAMPGROUNDS

Starrigavan Campground—.7 miles north of ferry dock. No water supply except creek. (Creek water should be boiled).Picnic tables, firepits, toilets. Spaces not drive-through. Free.

Sawmill Creek—14 miles from ferry, up Blue Lake Road, just past the pulp mill. Picnic tables, firepits, toilets. No water. Large spaces but none drive-through. Free.

LAUNDROMAT

Duds & Suds, 903 Halibut Point Rd. 747-5050. Shower. Open 8 a.m.–10 p.m.

The steeple of St. Michael's Cathedral stands above downtown Sitka in this view from Castle Hill.

BOATS

Information on fishing charters and charters to offshore bird rookeries with skippers licensed by the Coast Guard is available at the Centennial Building and from Sitka Bus Lines. Boat fuel at three fuel docks in Sitka Channel near Thomson Harbor. Boats can be moored overnight at certain stalls on floats in Thomson Harbor, Crescent Harbor behind Centennial Building. Contact the Harbormaster, VHF Channel 16 or 747-3294.

FACILITIES

PROPANE: **Service Transfer** on Lincoln St.

DIESEL: **Sitka Fuels** on Katlian St., **Chevron** station on Lake St.

ICE at canneries on Katlian St.

DUMPING STATION: **State Garage** on Halibut Point Rd.

OUTBOARD MOTOR REPAIR: across from ferry terminal at **Southeast Marine.** Also repair motorcycles.

HOSPITAL: **Sitka Community Hospital,** Halibut Point Rd. 747-3241.

PETS: Vet is Dr. Burgess Bauder. Office is behind the city garage on Halibut Point Rd., open 3 p.m.–5 p.m., Monday–Friday. 747-3056. No boarding facilities in town.

HAPPENINGS

Sitka Music Festival (chamber music) in Centennial Building, June 7–June 28, Tuesday and Friday evenings. Some of world's finest musicians perform.

Salmon Derby, Memorial Day weekend and first weekend in June.

All-Alaska Logging Championships, June 29–30, 1985.

Alaska Day Festival, Oct. 18, celebrating the Russian transfer of Alaska to the United States. Transfer is reenacted with period costumes, muskets and flags. Week-long celebration.

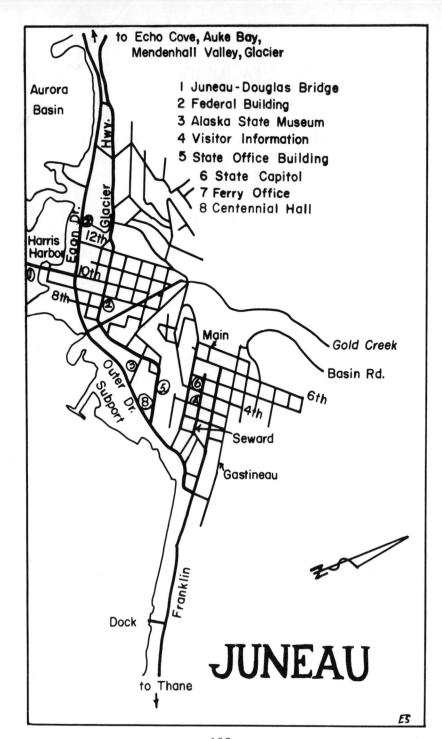

to Echo Cove, Auke Bay,
Mendenhall Valley, Glacier

Aurora Basin

1 Juneau-Douglas Bridge
2 Federal Building
3 Alaska State Museum
4 Visitor Information
5 State Office Building
6 State Capitol
7 Ferry Office
8 Centennial Hall

Hwy.

Glacier

Egan Dr.

Harris Harbor

12th

10th

8th

Outer Dr.

Subport

Main

Gold Creek

Basin Rd.

6th

4th

Seward

Gastineau

Franklin

Dock

JUNEAU

to Thane

N

ES

Downtown Juneau covers the shore of Gastineau Channel below 3576 ft. Mt. Juneau.

JUNEAU
(Area Code 907, Zip 99801,2,3,11)

JUNEAU (pop. of city and borough 29,000) is Alaska's state capital. It is nestled on the slopes between Gastineau Channel and Mounts Juneau and Roberts, which rise over 3,000 feet above the town. In 1880, prospectors Joe Juneau and Dick Harris were hired by geologist George Pilz to contact Chief Kowee and confirm the presence of gold. They found gold in what is now Gold Creek, and a mining camp sprang up, named Juneau in 1881.

Besides placer gold from the creeks, gold was mined in two deep shaft systems: the Alaska Juneau Mine, and the Treadwell Mine on Douglas Island (extending under Gastineau Channel). Over $66 million in gold was removed before gold mining was declared a "nonessential wartime activity" during World War II, and the Alaska-Juneau Mine was closed. The Treadwell was closed some years earlier when the shafts under the channel caved in and flooded with sea water.

109

As Juneau grew past Sitka in size and activity, the district capital in 1906, the territorial capital in 1912, and later the state capital, were established here. Distances in Alaska are so great that most state departments have additional offices in other towns as well.

Juneau has so little flat ground in the downtown area that building has extended northwest into the Mendenhall Valley, where most residents now live. A jet airport and the Mendenhall Glacier also occupy the valley.

Since the glaciers dump sediment carried by the Mendenhall River and Lemon Creek into the channel, ships cannot pass north of Juneau, and must go back down the channel and around Douglas Island. In order to avoid many miles of extra sailing, the ferries use a terminal at Auke Bay, 14 miles north of town. Distances are given from the **downtown docks** unless otherwise noted.

TO SEE AND DO

• Take a walking tour of downtown Juneau. Maps are available at the waterfront information center (Kiosk), most hotels, and the Juneau Visitor Information Center in the log cabin at 3rd and Seward Streets. The tour passes historic sites and buildings of interest on Juneau's hills and waterfront.

• Notice bald eagles on beaches, pilings, and trees around town and on the road north.

•Visit the Alaska State Museum, on Whittier St. Open 9 a.m. to 9 p.m. Mon.–Fri., 1 p.m. to 9 p.m. weekends in summer. Native culture, wildlife, historic exhibits, changing art exhibits. No charge. Donations accepted.

• See St. Nicholas Russian Orthodox Church, 326 5th St., built in 1894. Frame building, icons, artifacts. Guided tours in summer. Donation requested $1 per person.

• See the Mendenhall Glacier, 13 miles from downtown, 5 miles from Auke Bay ferry dock. Reach by car, bus tour, or municipal bus (Monday–Saturday, $.75, you must walk the last mile). You will find a U.S. Forest Service Visitors Center with programs, naturalists to answer your questions, nature walks, trails, and a good view of the glacier face. The Visitor Center is open weekends all year. From mid-May to September 30 it's open 9 a.m.–6 p.m., seven days a week. Sockeye (red) salmon spawn in the stream in July and August, arctic terns nest in the gravel, and you may even see mountain goats above by telescope.

• Auke Lake, 12 miles from downtown. Also the location of Chapel by-the-Lake, and the University of Alaska campus. Get there on bus tour, or on municipal bus (except Sundays). The chapel has a famous view of the Mendenhall Glacier across Auke Lake.

• Auke Bay Marine Lab, by car or municipal bus. Research lab has self-guided tour and exhibits, 9 a.m. to 4 p.m., weekdays.

• Auke Bay ferry terminal, 14 miles from downtown. In daylight, watch eagles, herons, a kingfisher who likes to dive off the dock, porpoises, seals, and an occasional whale. Eagles are often perched on the piling below the grocery store at Auke Bay small boat harbor.

• Fish by boat or from shore. For rental and fishing charter information ask at Visitor Information Center, 3rd and Seward. Beach fishing on Douglas Island, and north of Juneau.

• Fly over the Juneau Icefield. On a clear day this is an unforgettable experience. The Icefield, which feeds the Mendenhall Glacier, covers 1500 square miles, supplying 36 glaciers. Many spectacular peaks. Local plane charters run about $70 per person. **Temsco Helicopters**, adjacent to the airport 9 miles from town, will fly you to the ice and land you on it. 789-9501.

• Ride the Eaglecrest Ski Area chairlift up its 1400-foot climb for a grand view over subalpine landscapes on the way up, and coming down, Gastineau Channel, coastal mountains, glaciers and the edge of the Juneau Icefield. Every fifth chair is covered, to allow for changing weather. There are hiking trails and beautiful picnic spots at the top, a nature walk at the bottom with food, an information center and small gift shop in the ski lodge. Caution: if you do hike away from the top of the lift, please take a map and compass you know how to use, some emergency hiking gear, and be sure you know where you are going. **Grayline** runs tours with transportation from downtown Juneau. Memorial Day to Labor Day, seven days a week, 11 a.m.–7 p.m. Lift ride only, $10 round trip. 586-6464.

• State Office Building, 4th and Main. Free concerts on old theater pipe organ, Friday noons, in spectacular 8th floor lobby with totem and view over channel.

• Alaska Department of Fish and Game, 3/4 Mile Egan Drive, behind KINY Radio, has wildlife notebook series with information on all major land and water wildlife in Alaska.

• State Capitol Building, 4th between Seward and Main. Free tours daily in summer.

• Federal Building, Glacier Avenue and 9th, houses the offices of all federal agencies. Cooperative Extension Office, ground floor, off lobby has free or inexpensive leaflets on everything from rhubarb and sourdough recipes to how to tan hides with battery acid and salt! Bureau of Indian Affairs, 3rd floor, exhibit of native artifacts.

• Gold Creek Salmon Bake, at the end of Basin Rd. Courtesy bus picks visitors up at Baranof Hotel at 6 p.m. Music, entertainment. Operates nightly outdoors (under a roof), 6 p.m. to 9 p.m., May 28–September 10. All you can eat, $16.

• Ore House Salmon Bake, 4 miles south on Thane Road. Tickets available at the Baranof Hotel. Salmon, crab, halibut, BBQ ribs. Mining operation, gold panning, mining exhibit. Indoor and outdoor seating. Handicapped accessible. 5 p.m.–9 p.m., June 1–Sept. 30. 586-3567.

• Hike trails in Southeastern Alaska's most extensive system. Trail maps and guidebooks are available from the Forest Service, and commercially. The trail up Mt. Roberts (good view of town) begins at the end of 6th St. The trail up Mt. Juneau (requires respect for weather and snow on trail) starts beyond Salmon Bake Turnoff, at end of Basin Road. The trail to Pt. Bishop from end of Thane Road is 8 miles of flat hiking, through forest and along shore. Good camping and fishing at Dupont, 3 miles from start of trail. Free guide to Juneau area trails is available from U.S. Forest Service and Davis Log Cabin.

Juneau's Eagle Beach, the Chilkat Mountains and Lynn Canal.

• Drive your car or a rented one "out the road," a phrase Juneau-ites use to describe any place north of Auke Bay, for a picnic and beautiful view. Fire pits and picnic shelters (open with roofs for rain) at Auke Bay Recreation Area and Lena Cove. Fire pits at Eagle Beach. Pit toilets at all areas. Good picnicking and views from North Douglas Road. Some tourists drive these roads simply because they've never been where all the roads have ends!

• Ride the ferries on one day or overnight excursions if you're using Juneau as a base. On Tuesdays the *Taku* and on Wednesdays the *Malaspina* stay in Skagway all afternoon, making a good round trip from Juneau to Haines or Skagway for walk-on passengers (summer only).

• Join an adventure tour with **Alaska Travel Adventures**, 200 N. Franklin. (907) 586-6245. Trips range from three-hour float trips on the Mendenhall River to kayak and climbing trips all over Alaska.

• For kayak equipment, instruction, guiding, rentals, **Alaska Discovery**, 418 S. Franklin, 586-1911. Has rentals in Glacier Bay, Angoon, and Juneau.

• For small personalized tours of the rain forest without the rigors of a wilderness trip, early morning birdwalks, tours of art galleries to meet the artists, special tours arranged according to your interests, including van transportation, call **Alaska Up Close**, 789-9544. P.O. Box 2666, Juneau, 99803.

• For similar tours conducted in German, call **German Connection Fototour**, 780-4911. P.O. Box 2925, Juneau 99803.

• Enjoy Juneau Icefield flight and a salmon bake at fly-in **Taku Glacier Lodge**, 586-1281 and 1362. Leaves from seadrome in front of Merchants' Wharf June 1–September 21. $105.

• For plays and other entertainment, check with the Visitor Information Center, 134 3rd St., corner of 3rd and Seward. (907) 586-2201 or the information kiosk in Marine Park in summer. Dial 586-JUNO for a 24 hour recorded message of scheduled events.

Cruise ships *Sun Princess* and *Sagafiord* docked at Juneau.

INFORMATION AVAILABLE at Visitor Information Center in Davis Log Cabin, 134 3rd St., Juneau, AK 99801, 586-2201. To learn about current happenings in Juneau, dial 586-JUNO for a recorded message. Hiking, kayaking, and mountaineering trips and information at Foggy Mountain Shop, 171 Shattuck Way, across from Marine Park. Forest Service information desk in Centennial Hall, 101 Egan Dr., 586-7151, has films, slide shows, demonstrations, and makes Forest Service cabin reservations. Open 8:30 a.m.–6 p.m. daily Memorial Day to mid-September, 9:00 a.m.–5:30 p.m. Mon.–Fri. rest of the year. Information on Glacier Bay National Park in Federal Building, Room 615. Information kiosk in Marine Park, adjacent to the cruise ship dock, summers. There's also an information booth in the airport terminal during summer. A guide to the area with many interesting notes is "This is Juneau," by Mike Miller, available in Juneau shops.

TRANSPORTATION

FERRY: **Alaska Marine Highway**, daily in summer. Auke Bay terminal, 14 miles north. Ferry office for information, reservations, tickets, 1½ miles, 1590 Glacier Ave. For time of arrival it's best to call the terminal. Terminal opens an hour or two prior to arrival, otherwise the message is recorded. Reservations, 465-3941; daily recorded ferry arrivals 465-3940; Auke Bay terminal, 789-7453. Additional ticket office at Main and 3rd streets.

BUS: Runs Monday through Saturday. Route goes from downtown ferry terminal through town to airport and Auke Bay store, 1.9 miles from Auke Bay ferry terminal. Some buses go to Douglas. Hourly, 6 a.m. to 1 a.m., depending on route. Check schedule as some hours are omitted at night. Ask for the express bus schedule as well—it's separate.

Bus service between downtown and the Auke Bay ferry terminal and the airport is provided by the **Capital Connexion** vans, 780-4677. They pick up at most downtown hotels and meet all ferries and flights. Fare from Auke Bay to town is $6. It's complimentary to some downtown hotels if you have reservations. 780-4677.

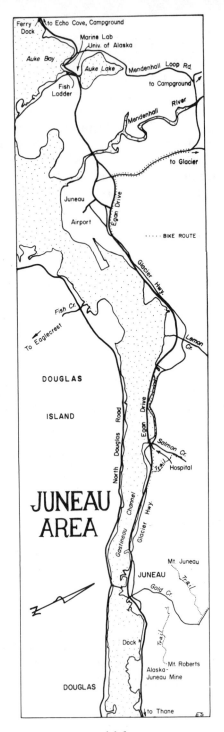

Ferry Dock / to Echo Cove, Campground

Marine Lab Univ. of Alaska

Auke Bay

Auke Lake

Mendenhall Loop Rd.

to Campground

Fish Ladder

Mendenhall River

to Glacier

Juneau Airport

Egan Drive

BIKE ROUTE

Glacier Hwy.

Fish Cr.

Lemon Cr.

To Eaglecrest

DOUGLAS

ISLAND

North Douglas Road

Egan Drive

Salmon Cr.

Trail

Hospital

JUNEAU AREA

Gastineau Channel

Glacier Hwy.

Mt. Juneau

Trail

JUNEAU

Gold Cr.

N

Trail

Dock

Mt. Roberts

Alaska-Juneau Mine

DOUGLAS

to Thane

ES

116

Contestants in 4th of July wheelbarrow race head up steep Franklin Street.

TAXI: **Glacier Taku Taxi,** 102 Franklin St., Juneau, 586-2121. **City Cab,** 321 Seward St., Juneau, 586-2200. Fare from town to Auke Bay terminal $14.

BUS TOURS: **Gray Line,** 586-3773, ticket desk in Baranof Hotel, June 1–September 30. Tours to glacier and around Juneau.

Northern Lights Sightseeing, 420 East St., Juneau 99801. 586-6471. Glacier and city tours. Meets some ferry arrivals.

CAR RENTAL: **Hertz,** Juneau Airport, 789-9494. **Avis,** Juneau Airport, 789-9450. **Payless Rent-a-Car,** Dawson's Automotive, Box 675, Juneau 99802, 586-2367. **National,** Juneau Airport, 789-9814. **Rent-A-Dent,** Hal Moore Motors in Airport Shopping Center, adjacent to Juneau Airport. P.O. Box 273, Auke Bay 99821. 789-9000. **Budget,** Juneau Airport, 789-5186. **Ugly Duckling,** 5000 Glacier Hwy. (Tides Motel), 586-2452.

AIR: **Alaska Airlines,** (907) 789-0600, to Ketchikan, Sitka, Gustavus, Petersburg, Wrangell, Anchorage, Fairbanks, Seattle, and other West Coast cities.

Western Airlines, (907) 789-5095, to Ketchikan (summer only), Fairbanks, Seattle, and routes in the "Lower 49."

Trans North Air, (907) 789-3262, to Whitehorse and other Yukon and Northwest Territories towns, all year. **Air North,** (907) 789-3535, to Whitehorse and Fairbanks, summers.

CHARTERS: Some operators have mail contracts requiring scheduled flights to other towns, on which you can ride at a flat rate (you don't have to charter the whole plane.) These are listed for some minor ports. **Channel Flying, Inc.,** 2601 Channel Dr., Juneau 99801, (907) 586-3331. **LAB Flying Service,** Terminal Building, Juneau Airport, Juneau 99803, (907) 789-9160. **Ward Air,** Terminal Building, Juneau Airport, 789-9150. **Wings of Alaska,** Terminal Building, Juneau Airport, 789-0790. Mailing address: 1873 Shell Simmons Dr., Suite 119, Juneau 99801. Scheduled service to Hoonah, Haines, Skagway. **Skagway Air Service,** Terminal Building, Juneau Airport, 789-2006. **Glacier Bay Airways,** Terminal Building, Juneau Airport, 789-9009.

BIKE ROUTE: A cycle path follows the Mendenhall Loop Road from near the glacier to Egan Drive and along it to the Old Glacier Hiway near Switzer Village. Another segment follows Old Glacier Hiway beside Twin Lakes from near Lemon Creek to Salmon Creek. From there a path follows north of Egan Drive to Glacier Highway in town. Thus it is possible to cycle from DeHart's Store at Auke Bay to Juneau without getting on the freeway. You'll want time and daylight the first time. Bicycle lanes also parallel some other main roads.

BAGGAGE STORAGE at hotels, for patrons, on day of departure. Auke Bay ferry terminal has some lockers, but is locked when ships aren't in. **Alaska Discovery,** 418 S. Franklin. Overnight storage fee. The new airport terminal expansion will have baggage storage lockers, starting in summer 1985. Outside, but under roof, baggage lockers are being discussed at the Auke Bay terminal.

Birdwatchers on the airport dike near Juneau watch ducks and geese on the Mendenhall Wetlands, a state game refuge.

HOTELS
(6% tax extra)

Alaskan Hotel—167 S. Franklin St., Juneau 99801. (907) 586-1000. Sauna, jacuzzi. Single w/o bath, $36. Single with shower, $50. Double $5 more. Add'l, $5 adult, $3 child. Kitchenettes extra. No pets.

Baranof Hotel—127 N. Franklin St., Juneau 99801. (907) 586-2660. Housekeeping units, restaurant, lounge, hair styling shop, travel agency, gift shop, coffee shop. Single $80–$86, Double $92–$98. Add'l, $15/person. No pets.

Bergmann Hotel—434 Third St., Juneau 99801. (907) 586-1690. Chinese restaurant, lounge, parking, cable TV. Single $37.45 incl. tax, Double and Twin $48.15, weekly rates. Housekeeping units available. No pets.

Best Western Country Lane Inn—9300 Glacier Hwy., Juneau 99801. (907) 789-5005, toll free reservations 1-800-528-1234, in Hawaii and Alaska 1-800-334-9401. 4 miles from Mendenhall Glacier, near airport. Courtesy transportation to airport, ferry, and downtown Juneau. Complimentary continental breakfast. Free local phone calls, cable TV with HBO. Indoor pool and jacuzzi. Room prices from $59 single to $96 for suites.

Breakwater Inn—1711 Glacier Avenue, Juneau 99801. (907) 586-6303. Mail: Box 1428, Juneau 99802. Dining room, lounge, beauty shop. Good view of waterfront, boat harbor. Single $65, Double $68. Add'l, $10/person. Deluxe unit add'l. Children under 12 free. Free transportation to downtown at scheduled times, June through September. No pets.

Driftwood Lodge—435 Willoughby Avenue, Juneau 99801. (907) 586-2280. Housekeeping units. Color TV, HBO. Single $45, Double $52. Add'l, $7/person. Small dogs allowed. No cats. Toll free number 800-544-2239.

Sheffield Juneau—51 West Egan Drive, Juneau 99801. 586-6900. Restaurant, lounge, dancing. Single $102, Double $112. Children under 18 free if in room with parent. Commercial and government rates (fill out application at desk). No pets.

Prospector Hotel—375 Whittier St., Juneau 99801. 586-3737. 60 rooms, restaurant, lounge, live entertainment five nights a week. Single $66, Double $74, Suites $86. Add'l, $8/person. Pets allowed with manager's okay.

Summit Hotel—455 S. Franklin St., Juneau, 586-2050. Single, $30–32 w/o bath, Double $32–34 w/o bath. Weekly rates. No pets. (1983 rates)

Super 8 Motel—Near airport. 2295 Trout St. (behind McDonald's). Juneau 99803. 789-4858. 75 rooms, cable TV, direct-dial phone, elevator, coin-op laundry, conference room. Queen-size beds, paraplegic room, courtesy continental breakfast. Courtesy transportation to airport and ferry. Pets with permission. Rooms from $51.88.

Tides Motel—5000 Glacier Hwy., Juneau, 99801, 586-2452. Across road from Grants Plaza with supermarket, gas, etc. Motel has restaurant, gift shop, washeteria, showers. Also has camper spaces with and without hookups, dump station. Single $54, Double $64. Housekeeping units extra. No pets.

Youth Hostel—Hill overlooking downtown Juneau. AYH. Open year-round beginning May 25, 1985. 614 Harris Street. 586-9559, P.O. Box 1543, Juneau, AK 99802. All ages welcome. Dormitory sleeping quarters, cooking facilities, showers, living room, dining area. Groups welcome. No pets, Register 5:00 p.m. to 11:00 p.m. Closed 9:00 a.m. to 5:00 p.m. Maximum stay, three nights. $6.50 AYH members, $8.50 non-AYH members.

Alaska Bed & Breakfast, 526 Seward St., Juneau 99801. 586-2959. Books people into private Juneau homes. Rates vary but average $35/Single, $45/Double. This office also handles reservations for homes in Wrangell, Petersburg, Sitka, Angoon, Elfin Cove, and Haines. Reservations suggested. Some homes do take pets.

Juneau's airport and the Mendenhall Glacier reflected in the floatplane pond.

CAMPGROUNDS

Mendenhall Lake—5 miles from Auke Bay dock, off Mendenhall Loop Road, 2 miles northwest of Visitor Center. USFS. $5 per day, June 1–September 15. May be open free a few days before and after according to snow. Great views of glacier, hiking. Some mosquitos. Firewood scarce and possibly green. Tables, fire grates, water, restrooms, central dump station. 60 spaces, some drive-through.

Auke Village Recreation Area—2 miles northwest of Auke Bay ferry terminal. USFS. $5 per day. 11 sites. Boating and beach adjacent. Fewer bugs. Same info as above, but no dump station.

With regret, I advise not leaving valuables in camp when you leave, and recommend marking equipment obviously and permanently with your name.

Aurora Basin Boat Harbor—parking for self-contained units. Must check-in with police, 210 Admiral Way. $2.50/night.

Douglas Shop-Rite Market, 1102 3rd St., Douglas, (907) 364-3414. 4 miles. Part of parking lot has electricity. Market (check-in) open till midnight daily. $6 w elec. Large spaces, none drive-through.

Glacier Highway—Tides Motel & Camper Park, 5000 Glacier Hwy., (907) 586-2452. Spaces with and without hookups. $10 with hookups, $5 without.

LAUNDROMATS

Harbor Wash Board, 1111 F. St., Juneau, off Glacier Ave., behind Alaska Laundry, also has showers. There are several others in the area. Near the airport, there is one behind **Mini Mall** (photo), on Old Glacier Highway. **The Dungeon** is in basement of the Mendenhall Apartments on North Franklin St. On Mendenhall Loop Road, between Egan Drive and the glacier, **Thunder Mt.** trailer park has a laundromat on Thunder Mt. Road. **Portside Laundromat**, in the Breakwater Inn's basement, 1711 Glacier Ave., also has showers.

FACILITIES

SWIMMING POOL: **Augustus Brown Pool** at Juneau-Douglas High School on Glacier Avenue has open hours, weight equipment, a sauna, and showers.

DUMP STATION: **Tides Motel** on Glacier Highway, **Mendenhall Campground, City-Borough** shops in Douglas at 3rd and Front St.

PROPANE: **Petrolane Alaska Gas Service,** 3850 Mendenhall Loop Rd. (road to glacier). **Valley Chevron** in Mendenhall Shopping Center. **Aurora Basin** fuel dock.

DIESEL: **Ray Emig's Chevron,** 10th St. **Valley Chevron** in Mendenhall Shopping Center. **Gas 'N Go,** Grant's Plaza on Glacier Highway at Lemon Creek. **Airport Union,** Glacier Hwy. & Airport Rd. **Aurora Basin** fuel dock.

ICE: All supermarkets. **Breeze Inn,** convenience late night grocery, Glacier Hwy. and Trout St.

HOSPITAL: **Bartlett Memorial Hospital,** 3½ miles, Glacier Highway, 586-2611. Ambulance, fire department, dial 911.

PETS: Veterinarians, **Southeast Alaska Veterinary Clinic,** 7691. Glacier Hwy., Juneau 99801. 789-7551. Boarding, **Gastineau Humane Society,** 7705 Glacier Hwy., Juneau 99801. 789-0260.

BOATS

CHARTERS: **Bay of Three Rivers,** Glen Byrns, Box 453, Juneau 99802, (907) 789-9845. Scenic river tours, fishing, hunting.

Other licensed charter operators available through Visitor Information Center. Boats can be hired for Tracy Arm (a spectacular fiord with glaciers), Berners Bay, Taku Inlet, or for good fishing. Airboat charters into Berners Bay are also available.

BOAT TOURS: **Alaska Exploration Holidays** (to Glacier Bay), 76 Egan Dr., Juneau 99801. 586-6883. Regularly scheduled tours to Glacier Bay.

Riviera Cruises, 14 Marine Way, Juneau 99801, (907) 586-9888. Daily 10-hour cruises to Tracy Arm and shorter fly cruises using floatplane to meet the boat at Tracy Arm. Some cruises in winter.

FUEL AND MOORAGE at Aurora Basin, Harris Harbor, Douglas and Auke Bay. Dock space limited, especially in summer.

HAPPENINGS

Salmon Derby, August 9–11, 1985. Big prizes.

GLACIER BAY NATIONAL PARK

THIS SPECTACULAR 45-60-mile-long bay is fed by a dozen glaciers at its upper end. It has bears, seals, whales, tufted puffins, and lots of icebergs. Many seabirds come ashore only to nest here.

The park is some distance by boat or plane from Juneau—there is no ferry service. The glaciers are 45 miles from the airport and park headquarters near Gustavus. You may get there using the following:

• A chartered flight over the bay from Juneau, Haines, or Skagway or to Gustavus. Flights are cheapest from Haines, but the clouds must be high enough for the plane to get over the mountains, or at least between them.

• The **Alaska Airlines** air-boat tour from Juneau. This can include a night at Glacier Bay Lodge, round trip boat service to the glacier with a Park Service naturalist, and return flight to Juneau, May 24–Sept. 22. Air fare alone is $89 super saver, or $120 standard fare round trip from Juneau. Does not include airport transfers at Juneau and Gustavus. Additional nights at the lodge can be added, as well as an overnight near a glacier on an excursion boat with staterooms. For package prices contact the airline or tour operators below.

• **Glacier Bay Airways**, Box 1, Gustavus, Alaska 99826. 697-2249, in Gustavus. 789-9009, in Juneau Airport. Scheduled air service between Juneau and Gustavus. Air charter service to Juneau, Haines, other Southeastern points. Sometimes is the cheapest way to move a group of people, boats, gear. Also does flightseeing in the park from Bartlett Cove.

• **Glacier Bay Yacht Tours:** 2 and 3 day package tours from Juneau by boat. Some flying is involved in the shorter packages. These tours are scheduled several times weekly in the summer. 76 Egan Drive, Suite 110, near Merchants' Wharf. Juneau, 99801. (907) 586-6835. $219–379. Off-season rates for groups. Will drop off and pick up campers. Daily boat service between Juneau and Gustavus in summer 1985.

• **Alaska Exploration Holidays & Cruises,** same office as above, different boats. 76 Egan Drive, Suite 110, Juneau 99801. 586-6835, 586-6883. Call toll-free 800-426-0600. Have one-day tour, flying over from Juneau, cruising the bay to the glaciers, and flying back to Juneau, $225, June 1–Sept. 15. Resort tour, two days, one night in lodge, boat tour to glaciers, round trip Juneau to Bartlett Cove, May 24–Sept. 22, from $268. Includes everything except meals. Other tours include a night on boat with staterooms near a glacier.

• Charter a boat from Juneau (if you can get enough people). This can be cheaper than the package deals, which all run over $100 per person.

One option, if you do get to park headquarters at Bartlett Cove, is to take camping gear and a small boat or kayak "up-bay" on the concessioner's boat. For a small additional fee, you can be let off where you choose, and picked up some days later. Instead, you may want to camp and paddle your way back down the bay to Bartlett Cove. You can thereby have a longer trip in this wild area for only a bit more than the overnight trip. There is no extra charge for kayaks taken as hand luggage on the ferry to Juneau, but they are difficult to hitch with around town. Taku Taxi in Juneau will carry them on top. Kayaks are available for rent in Gustavus, so you don't have to bring your own.

• The Park Service has a helpful information sheet for back country users and conducts an orientation session for kayakers at 6 p.m. nightly at Bartlett Cove in summer. Kayaks getting dropped off the following day are loaded on the *Thunder Bay* at the session.

A day in Glacier Bay with a Park Service naturalist is included in the itinerary of most of the cruise ships running in Southeastern Alaska.

Some air-boat packages as well as some of the charter boat trips include an overnight anchored near one of the glaciers.

FOR INFORMATION about the park, write National Park Service, Gustavus, AK 99826, (907) 697-2237. Good people to call for bear information, and suggestions for trips at all times especially during off-season, when the lodge is closed and excursion boat and some flights aren't running.

HOTELS

Glacier Bay Lodge—Box 108, Gustavus, AK 99826, 697-3221. For info and reservations all year: 1500 Metropolitan Park Bldg., Seattle, WA 98101. (206) 624-8551 in Washington State. Toll-free from rest of U.S., (800) 426-0600. Open May 24–Sept. 22, 1985. Dining room, lounge, gift shop, charter fishing, boat rentals, flightseeing, boat fuel. Package tour available from Juneau. Lodge only, $49 per person, twin occupancy. Children's rates, extra nights available. Have package tour with overnight on boat near glaciers.

Gustavus Inn—Box 31, Gustavus, AK 99826. Summer (907) 697-2254, Winter (907) 586-2006. Open March 1–Oct. 1. Family, farm style. Rooms for 20 guests. Meals are famous, featuring home-grown produce, local seafood. Located one mile from airport on road to monument. Glacier Bay kayaking and charter fishing available. Rates $80/person twin occupancy, includes airport transfer, meals, use of bicycles and sport fishing gear. All-inclusive tour, one night/two days, $280, includes round trip air fare from Juneau, all meals, room at inn, all transfers, and Thunder Bay day boat tour to glaciers.

Salmon River Cabin Rentals—Box 13, Gustavus, AK 99826, (907) 697-2245. Housekeeping cabins, close to good fishing. Sleeping bag and bicycle rentals. Walking distance from beach. Bus service to Glacier Bay Nat'l Park. Cabin for 1 to 4 persons, $40/day, $200/week. Free transportation to and from airport.

CAMPGROUNDS

Bartlett Cove, in park. Walking distance from lodge, on shore. Tables, pit toilets. Seals and whales often just offshore. You can sometimes buy fresh seafood from commercial fishing boats at the dock. Pets allowed in Bartlett Cove area on leash. Not allowed in back country.

BOATS

EXCURSION boat cruise on *M/V Thunder Bay*, $99.50 round-trip to glacier.

MOORAGE, but no dock space, fuel, skiff rentals at Bartlett Cove. Engine repair, Honda dealer in Gustavus. Private boats need permit to enter park.

KAYAK rentals in Gustavus as well as guided trips, **Alaska Discovery**, (907) 697-2257.

FACILITIES

GROCERY STORE: Gustavus now has a small grocery store.

AIRFIELD: Runways at Gustavus Airport 7,500' and 5,000' paved. No fuel. Radio 122.5 to Juneau on field.

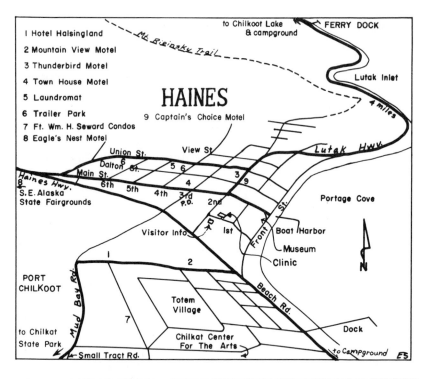

1 Hotel Halsingland
2 Mountain View Motel
3 Thunderbird Motel
4 Town House Motel
5 Laundromat
6 Trailer Park
7 Ft. Wm. H. Seward Condos
8 Eagle's Nest Motel

9 Captain's Choice Motel

HAINES

to Chilkoot Lake & campground

FERRY DOCK

Mt. Bieinsku Trail

Lutak Inlet

4 miles

Lutak Hwy.

View St.

Union St.

Dalton St.

Main St.

Haines Hwy.

6th   5th   4th   3rd

S.E. Alaska
State Fairgrounds

P.O.

2nd

1st

Front St.

Portage Cove

Boat Harbor

Museum

Clinic

Visitor Info.

PORT
CHILKOOT

to Chilkat
State Park

Mud Bay Rd.

Small Tract Rd.

1

2

7

Totem
Village

Chilkat Center
For The Arts

Beach Rd.

Dock

to Campground

N

ES

Port Chilkoot, formerly Ft. William H. Seward, in winter.

128

HAINES
(Area Code 907, Zip Code 99827)

CHILKAT INDIANS lived in this area and traded with inland natives long before John Muir and S. Hall Young arrived in 1879 and selected it as a mission site. The mission was established in 1881, followed by salmon canneries, mining, and an army post in 1903. During the Klondike Rush this was the southern end of the Dalton Trail, a toll road over which stock could be driven to supply meat to the northern settlements. The Haines Highway, connecting the Inside Passage with the Alaska Highway, generally follows the Dalton Trail. Today, Haines (pop. 1,847) has a sawmill, a large fishing fleet, and the hotels and other tourist facilities that mark the end of the Marine Highway and the beginning of the land road to interior Alaska. Near the ferry docks, a tank farm marks the end of a six-inch oil pipeline to Fairbanks, built in 1953 and now in dead storage.

Bald eagles are a big attraction at the Chilkat Bald Eagle Preserve along the Chilkat River flats near Mile 19 out of Haines, in fall and winter. The river has warm springs running into it, so it never freezes, thereby providing the eagles with a dependable food supply. The largest known congregation of bald eagles meets here to fish and spend hours perched in snowy trees along the highway. Over 3,000 have been counted here in a single day! November is the peak month, but you will see many from October through February.

TO SEE AND DO

• Tour Fort William H. Seward, 5 miles from ferry, just south of town. Walking-tour brochures are available at hotels and the Chamber of Commerce.

• Visit the Alaska Indian Arts workshop and totem village (on walking tour). Watch totem carving, and purchase crafts made here.

• See the Chilkat Indian dancers in authentic costumes. Chilkat Center for the Arts, performing Tues., Thurs., and Sat. at 8:30 p.m. Adults $5, children $3.50. Five miles from ferry at Ft. William H. Seward. Performances in Port Chilkoot Tribal

House by appointment. Ask at the Visitor Information Center or Chilkat Center.

• See melodrama "Lust for Dust or Patience Rewarded," at Chilkat Center for the Arts, Fri. and Sun., 8:30 p.m. Adults $4, children $2.

• Enjoy a salmon bake over alderwood fire, served in the Chilkat Raven tribal house, Port Chilkoot. All you can eat. Beer and wine served. Daily, June through August, 5 p.m.–8 p.m. Information at Hotel Halsingland, 766-2000.

• Visit Sheldon Museum, 5 miles from ferry, Main St., in new building. Historic and native artifacts, changing exhibits, open daily, 1–4 p.m., Mon.–Sat., and by appointment. Call Lib Hakkinen, 766-2366. $2 adults over 18.

• Walk down to the boat harbor where 65 fishing boats are based, all year, in addition to several hundred during fishing season. Watch fishermen mending nets and get a close-up look at the different types of boats and gear used in Alaska.

• Watch salmon pass fish weir in the Chilkoot River, below Chilkoot Lake, about 4½ miles north (to the right) of the ferry terminal. June through October.

• See Davidson Glacier from Mud Bay Rd., and Rainbow Glacier (hanging) from farther down Mud Bay Rd.

• Fish in Lynn Canal and Chilkat River for salmon, and in Chilkoot Lake for trout. Five miles from ferry.

• Watch bald eagles at the 48,000-acre Chilkat Bald Eagle Preserve on the Chilkat River flats along the Haines Highway. Eagles are there October through February, with greatest numbers between Miles 19 and 22 from Haines. Truck traffic along the narrow road is fast, so one should use the pullouts which are good eagle-watching view-points. The eagles will be disturbed and fly away when approached closely, but you can watch easily from the pullouts and get good photos with any sort of telephoto lens. If not disturbed, eagles will perch for hours on the same branch, making photography easy. Dress warmly and bring a hot thermos. Rental cars are available in Haines if you don't bring your own.

• Hike the trail up Mt. Ripinsky for a grand view down Lynn Canal and over surrounding mountains.

• Visit Chilkat State Park on Mud Bay Road. Visitor Center, camping, picnicking, boat launch, dock, trails. Some programs in summer. Dates open according to snow. Great scenery.

• See old salmon cannery at Letnikof Cove on Mud Bay Road.

• Hike trails on Chilkat Peninsula. "Haines is for Hikers" brochure, available at Chamber of Commerce—Visitor Info Center.

• Fly over Glacier Bay and the Juneau Icefields.

• Tour Haines by bus on longer ferry stops. Most southbound ferries in 1985 stop in Haines at least two hours. Though the dock is five miles from town, there is bus service and time for shopping or a tour if you have boarded at Skagway. Bus meets ferries.

INFORMATION AVAILABLE at the Chamber of Commerce Building, 2nd and Willard St., downtown. Haines Visitor Center and Chamber of Commerce, P.O. Box 518, Haines, 99827. 766-2202. 10 a.m.–8 p.m., June 1–August 31. Shorter winter hours. U.S. Forest Service and Alaska State Parks will have a summer office, location undetermined at press time.

TRANSPORTATION

FERRY: **Alaska Marine Highway**. Ships run daily in summer. Dock is five miles north of town on Lutak Inlet.

BUS: Runs to and from ferry dock and airport. Stops at all hotels. **Travelot**, 766-2040, also has tours of Haines and Fort Wm. H. Seward during ferry stops.

Alaska-Yukon Motorcoaches to Fairbanks, Anchorage, Valdez, McKinley Park. Picks up at Hotel Halsingland, Haines, 766-2435. Anchorage (907) 276-1305. Seattle—Alaska Tour & Marketing, Suite 555, 4th & Battery Building, Seattle, WA 98121, (206) 682-4101, or toll-free from U.S. including Alaska, (800) 426-0600.

White Pass & Yukon Motorcoaches to Tok, Glennallen, Anchorage, Whitehorse. Ferry dock (meets Seattle ship), and 277 Main St. downtown. Mail: Box 601, Haines 99827. 766-2468. Divisoin of Westours. Toll-free in cont. U.S., (800) 544-2206. Trips are not daily, so it's best to call for info.

BUS TOURS (local): **Alaska Sightseeing,** office in Hotel Halsingland, 766-2000. **Travelot,** 766-2040. Has minivan.

TAXI: **Travelot,** 766-2040.

CAR RENTALS: **National Car Rental,** Eagle's Nest Motel, 766-2352. **Hertz,** Thunderbird Motel, 766-2131.

AIR: **LAB Flying Service,** Box 272, Haines 99827, (907) 766-2222. Juneau office. **Wings of Alaska** (scheduled carrier and charters). Haines office: 766-2468. Juneau office: 789-0790.

BAGGAGE STORAGE at hotels for patrons, on day of departure. Also at ferry terminal.

HOTELS
Bus stops at all hotels en route to ferry.
Sales tax 4% additional
(*1984 rates last reported.)

Captain's Choice Motel—5 miles, corner 2nd and Dalton. 22 rooms. TV, HBO, telephone, courtesy coffee, view of Lynn Canal. Box 392, Haines. 766-2461. Single $55, Double $60, Twin $65, Triple with double beds $75, Executive suite $85–$100. Pets allowed, some rooms.

Eagle's Nest Motel—6 miles from ferry, 3½ miles from airport. Haines Highway at Sawmill Rd. Box 267, Haines. 766-2352. 10 rooms, 2 family size, 8 doubles, all with queen-sized beds. Newly remodeled, color TV, HBO, courtesy coffee. Single $48, Double $54–65. Family rates. Walking distance to downtown, on Hwy. 7. Pets allowed.

Ft. Seward Bed & Breakfast—5½ miles from ferry, in Port Chilkoot. House #1 Seward Drive. Mail: Box 5, Haines 99827. 766-2856. Bed and breakfast inn in former officers' quarters. Sourdough hotcakes. Single $45, Double $55. No pets.*

Ft. Seward Condos—5½ miles from ferry in Port Chilkoot. Gregg Enterprises, Box 75, Haines, 766-2425, 766-2801. Converted apartments in officers' quarters at historic Ft. Wm. H. Seward. 1 and 2 bedrooms, some with fireplaces, overlooking bay and mountains, fully equipped kitchens. $60 per day (3 day min.), $400 per week.

Hotel Halsingland—5½ miles from ferry, in Port Chilkoot, Box 158, Haines, 766-2000. CB KFQ 0482. 60 rooms, 48 with bath. Dining room, cocktail lounge, salmon bake. Building was formerly the commanding officer's house in Ft. Wm. H. Seward. Single $48.50, Double $54.50, Triple $61.50, Quadruple $68.50. Economy rooms with shared bath. Pets allowed.*

Mountain View Motel—5½ miles from ferry, 151 Mud Bay Rd., Port Chilkoot. Mail: Box 62, Haines, 766-2900. Seven housekeeping units. TV, HBO. Single $45, Double $51. Open all year. Pets allowed.

Thunderbird Motel—5 miles from ferry, Dalton and 2nd. Mail: Box 159, Haines, 766-2131. 20 units (6 have kitchenettes), restaurant and bar around corner on 2nd. Phone, TV. Small pets allowed. Single $44, Double $51, Twin $56.*

Town House Motel—5 miles from ferry, 3rd and Main, Box 66, Haines 99827. (907) 766-2353. 24 units (6 are motel units, open all year; rest are trailer units, open May–Sept. 15), courtesy coffee, TV in motel units. Single $26–30, Double $32–34. No pets.*

Youth Hostel—6 miles from ferry, 1½ miles from post office on Small Tract Rd. **Bear Creek Camp**, Box 334, Haines. (907) 766-2259. All year. Sauna, woodstoves, cooking facilities, tent camping, trailer parking with hookups. Room for 20 in dorms. $7 in summer, $10 winter, Oct. 1–April 1, AYH. 2 family cabins. No pets.*

Totems and mountains on a sunny day in Haines.

Parking for self-contained RVs. Breakfast and dinner available. Tent space.

Cache Inn Lodge Cabins—6 miles from ferry. Mile 1 Mud Bay Road. P.O. Box 1045, Haines 99827. 766-2910. Rustic cabins with loft (sleep one to eight) facing Chilkat Inlet. Woodstove for cooking, dishes, pots, maid service. Bath house with showers and electricity. $30/cabin singles and seniors, $35/cabin for 3-4 people, $5/Add'l person. Weekly rates.

CAMPGROUNDS

STATE: **Chilkat State Park**—7 miles, Mud Bay Road. 40 vehicle spaces and 12 hike-in-camper spaces. Boat launch, dock. Tent pads, picnic tables, fireplaces, restrooms, water. Open dates according to snow. Note that the land just outside the entrance is private and camping is *not* allowed on it.

Chilkoot Lake—5 miles to right of ferry dock on Lutak Road; 10 miles from town. 38 spaces.

Portage Cove—2 miles from town, 7 miles from ferry, on Beach Road. Limited spaces. Tent campers and picknickers. No RVs.

Mosquito Lake Campground—32 miles from ferry, Mile 27 Haines Highway. 11 spaces.

All state campgrounds in Alaska are free, though a bill before the state legislature could establish overnight fees.

PRIVATE: **Port Chilkoot Camper Park**—5½ miles from ferry, Port Chilkoot. All facilities, showers, laundromat. 20 spaces with hookups. (Rates unknown)

PARKING is allowed off pavement toward town from dock along first 1/4 mile of road (though not recommended due to chance of vandalism). Over-night parking is done here "all the time."

FACILITIES

ICE: **Food Center, Alaska Liquor Store, Howser's Supermarket, Pioneer Bar & Liquor Store.**

PROPANE: **Eagle Transport, 790 Union St.**

DIESEL FUEL: **Valley Fuel Service** (50 gal. minimum), **Chevron, Wallace Garage, B & J Auto** (1 mi. Haines Hwy.).

CAR WASH: **Haines Auto Service Center,** 2nd and View Streets. Also **Tom's Self-Serv Car Wash,** Union and Main St.

DUMP STATION **Chevron,** Haines Hwy. and 3rd across from City Hall. $3 or free with 20 gal. gas purchase.

CLINIC: **Chilkat Valley Medical Center,** 766-2521, South 2nd St., doctors, nurses, dentist.

HORSE STALLS & EXERCISE AREA: Three transient box stalls available, more by arrangement. $5/night, negotiable if left clean. Riding arena. (907) 766-2476, or 2478 in mornings, or Linda Matthews, (907) 766-2163 at other hours. Southeast

Alaska Fairgrounds at southwest edge of town. For those vanning horses between South Central Alaska and the Lower 48, this is probably the best place en route to give them a break.

LAUNDROMATS

Port Chilkoot Camper Park—Port Chilkoot, 10 a.m. to 10 p.m. **Polyclean**—5th and Union, 10 a.m. to 10 p.m. Does dry cleaning. **Susie Q's**—Main St., across from museum. Have showers.

BOATS

Launching facilities at small boat harbor. Fuel available. For charters see Visitor Center or harbor bulletin board.

RIVER RAFT TOURS: There are several operators working out of Haines in summer. **Alaska River Expeditions** specializes in raft trips on the Arctic North Slope, and runs two day trips on the Tsirku River near Haines. Box G, Haines 99827. (907) 766-2409.

HAPPENINGS

Salmon Derby, Memorial Day weekend (3 days) and first weekend in June.

Southeast Alaska State Fair at the fairgrounds on the southwest edge of town, August 16–18, 1985 horse show August 15.

Haines has a growing number of artists whose work is displayed in local stores and studios. Theatrical and other cultural productions are done well and taken seriously here.

CUSTOMS: U.S. and Canadian customs stations are about 40 miles out of Haines on the Haines Hwy. They are closed from midnight to 8 a.m. and there are no facilities in the area. Requirements for Canadian customs are described at the end of the Prince Rupert section.

Mt. Ripinsky looks down on Haines—a good trail hike on a day like this!

UP THE HIGHWAY (THE LAND ONE!)

From Haines it's 775 miles to Anchorage and 653 miles to Fairbanks. Most of the Canadian part is gravel. The Klondike Highway from Skagway to Whitehorse is also gravel. Even in summer, you will enjoy the trip more as well as be safer if you don't try to hurry, but drive at reasonable speed, allowing for wildlife around the next bend. At night those animals are hard to see. Drive a reasonable number of hours per day and pull off to enjoy views or rest. Gas stations and mechanical service are a long way apart. Carry a few spares and basic tools as well as the service manual for your car. Screen protection for your headlights and radiator from flying rocks is recommended. So are a tow chain, flares, and extra water and fuel cans (which are best filled after you get off the ferry as they can't be stored on your car on the ship).

137

In winter all the above precautions apply, plus others. Think of Wyoming in January for driving conditions. Avoid driving in storms which can lead to white-out conditions and at night when unlit moose find the road an easy trail. With short daylight, you will probably drive some hours in the dark, but be careful. The RCMP, Alaska State Troopers and the ferry terminals have latest road conditions. If the weather ahead is awful when you get to Haines, your best bet is to wait a day or more.

Be **sure** your car is in good condition for cold weather driving, with good studded snow tires or chains, plenty of antifreeze, winter oil, and an engine block heater. Carry a flashlight and spare batteries and shovel and something for traction such as sand, kitty litter, burlap sacks, or pieces of expanded metal screen to put under spinning tires. Have plenty of warm clothes and sleeping bags for everyone in the car. Be prepared to spend the night in the car without running the engine for heat and carbon monoxide, and to be able to walk a few miles for help (if it's more than a very few or there are any vehicles coming by, don't walk). Keep your gas tank full as bad conditions can force you to drive for miles in low gear. Allow enough time for the drive and take more if needed to keep from driving while tired.

Driving to or from Prince Rupert in winter requires the same planning. In rare winters the road may be intermittently closed or cars led through in convoys due to avalanches on the highway between Smithers and Prince Rupert. Keep your speed down on this scenic 2-lane paved road and be prepared for several well-marked sharp turns the road makes across the railroad tracks. It's easy to forget while negotiating those turns to look for the occasional train as well! If you pull off at scenic points, you'll enjoy one of the more beautiful drives in the world.

Skagway Harbor and dock with the *Malaspina* and a cruise ship in port.

Skagway's new campground, Pullen Park (background), is very near the boat harbor and ferry terminal.

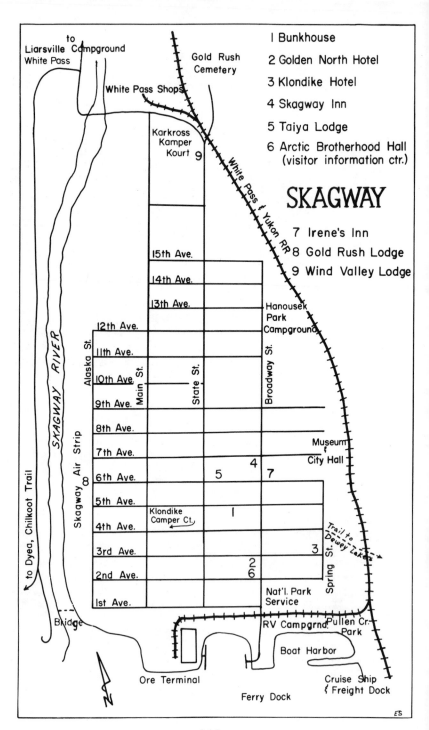

1 Bunkhouse
2 Golden North Hotel
3 Klondike Hotel
4 Skagway Inn
5 Taiya Lodge
6 Arctic Brotherhood Hall
   (visitor information ctr.)

SKAGWAY

7 Irene's Inn
8 Gold Rush Lodge
9 Wind Valley Lodge

to Liarsville Campground
White Pass

Gold Rush Cemetery

White Pass Shops

Karkross Kamper Kourt 9

White Pass & Yukon RR

15th Ave.
14th Ave.
13th Ave.
12th Ave.
11th Ave.
10th Ave.
9th Ave.
8th Ave.
7th Ave.
6th Ave.
5th Ave.
4th Ave.
3rd Ave.
2nd Ave.
1st Ave.

Alaska St.
Main St.
State St.
Broadway St.
Spring St.

SKAGWAY RIVER

to Dyea, Chilkoot Trail

Skagway Air Strip

8

Hanousek Park Campground

Museum
City Hall

4
5
7

Klondike Camper Ct.
1

3
Trail to Dewey Lakes

2
6

Nat'l. Park Service

Bridge

RV Campgrnd.

Pullen Cr. Park

Boat Harbor

Ore Terminal

Ferry Dock

Cruise Ship
& Freight Dock

N

ES

140

Skagway's historic district looking up Broadway, recently paved.

SKAGWAY
(Area Code 907, Zip Code 99840)

SKAGWAY (pop. 700) was founded in 1888 when Captain William Moore and his son settled here. They were overrun by the stampede to the Klondike in 1897. Skagway is at the head of the Taiya Inlet, the northern end of the Inside Passage, and the south end of the White Pass Route. Skagway and the ghost town of Dyea both served the Chilkoot Trail, and mushroomed into tent and clapboard cities during the winter of 1897–98. Later, when the White Pass and Yukon Railroad was built, Dyea died and Skagway became the main gateway to the Klondike, over 500 miles to the north. In Skagway, Soapy Smith, the notorious con artist, and his gang were expert at separating prospectors from their money and goods. Today the town lives on its historic past, with a good museum and many original buildings, as well as an ore terminal and the southern end of the White Pass and

141

Yukon Railroad. Most groceries and supplies headed for the Yukon and northern British Columbia are transferred from ship to train here. Metallic ore concentrate, shipped by rail from the Yukon, is put onto ships here (at the blue building near the ferry dock). In 1976 Klondike National Park was established, including the Chilkoot and White Pass trails, and most of Broadway (the main street of Skagway).

The Klondike Highway is open May 15 to September 15, sometimes later, over White Pass to Carcross and on to Whitehorse. For 67 miles it climbs to an altitude of 3290 feet along the route of the Klondike gold seekers. The scenery is fabulous, the surface is gravel. Customs is open from 8 a.m. to midnight near the summit. You can connect with the Alaska Highway near Whitehorse. There is fishing at lakes along the way if you have the appropriate British Columbia or Yukon fishing license. At stops to enjoy the view, you can also enjoy the tiny alpine tundra flowers at your feet.

There are several good spots to camp or picnic between the summit and Carcross. There are no facilities other than the customs station between Skagway and Carcross. It is about 31 miles from Carcross on to Whitehorse.

TO SEE AND DO

• Explore historic streets and buildings left from the Gold Rush days.

• Stop at the restored railroad depot on 1st Avenue for exhibits and programs by the National Park Service. Films and talks are given several times daily in summer, as are walking tours of historic features in Skagway.

• Visit the museum on 7th Avenue, 1 block east of Broadway. 8 a.m.–8 p.m., 7 days a week in summer. Donation, $2.

• See the "Days of '98 Show" in Eagle's Hall, Broadway and 6th. Adults $8, children $3. Daily mid-May to mid-September, fun gambling starts at 8 p.m., the show at 9 p.m. Matinee performances and sometimes morning shows on cruise ship days. No gambling at these shows. For times see the board in front of the hall or ask at the visitor information center in Arctic Brotherhood Hall. Jim Richards as Soapy Smith should *not* be missed.!

• In 1985, most ferries stop long enough in Skagway for a walk around town. Some stops are long enough for a drive to Dyea and the Chilkoot trailhead. I'd wait and see what time the ship actually arrives before counting on that if you are riding back on the same ship. The long stops make this a good one-day excursion from Juneau, especially on Tuesday and Wednesday in summer.

• Tour Skagway in 1890s style by pony taxi and buggy. **Skagway Hack.** (907) 983-2472. You can flag them down anywhere in town or find them standing outside the ferry terminal when the ship docks. These registered Welsh ponies and their entertaining drivers are fun!

• See both bald and golden eagles in the area. Swans sometimes stop near Dyea during migration.

• Fish Taiya Inlet, Skagway and Dyea rivers, and Dewey Lakes. Salt water fishing is generally better than lake fishing here. Dolly Varden in May and June, and salmon and halibut have all been caught from shore, dock or skiff very near the ferry dock. Ask the locals and remember to get a license even for salt water fishing.

• Visit Dyea, the takeoff point for the Chilkoot Pass. See the remains of buildings, boats, and the slide cemetery (for victims of the avalanche on the Chilkoot Trail in 1898). **Westours**, at the Klondike Inn, and **Klondike Safaris** offer bus service.

• See the Gold Rush cemetery at the north end of Skagway, with the graves of Soapy Smith and Frank Reid.

• Hike up to Dewey Lakes 1/4 mile, Reid Falls 1/2 mile, and Icy Lake 2 miles. Beautiful views and forest.

• Walk over the new footbridge across the Skagway River and follow the trail to Yakutania Point for a short, level hike to a good picnic spot.

• Backpack the historic and strenuous 33-mile Chilkoot Trail. Information on trail conditions is available from the National Park Service. Additional comments and suggestions on hiking the Chilkoot Trail are in the next section.

• Take a day bus tour over White Pass to Carcross and back or overnight to Whitehorse. The scenery and history combine to make this a great trip.

• Hope fervently with the rest of us that the White Pass & Yukon train will run again. The train, the historic route and scenery are a world class experience no one could forget.

INFORMATION AVAILABLE at the **National Park Service Visitor Center** in the restored railroad depot on 1st Ave., one block to the right at the first intersection. 983-2400 all year, 983-2518 in summer. The Park Service has the latest information on Chilkoot trail conditions and U.S. and Canadian regulation of the trail. They have good maps. Open 8 a.m.–8 p.m. in summer.

TRANSPORTATION

FERRY: **Alaska Marine Highway**, daily in summer. Dock is at south end of Broadway.

BUS: No public system yet.

TAXI: **Golden North**, 983-2451. **Sourdough Taxi, Goldie's Taxi**, 983-2321, also do tours. All charge about $2/person, ferry to town.

TOURS: **Atlas Tours**, summer, Golden North Hotel, 983-2402; winter, Box 4340, Whitehorse, Yukon, Canada Y1A 3T5. (403) 668-3161. **Golden North Taxi**, from Golden North Hotel. **Westours**, at Klondike Inn. **Skagway Travel** 983-2500, runs taxi to Chilkoot Trail head.

All these operators run tours around Skagway, to Dyea and to Carcross and Whitehorse.

CAR RENTAL: **Totem Car Rental**, P.O. Box 511, Skagway 99840, 983-2466. **Avis**, 983-2247. **Skagway Car Rental**, 983-2500.

RAIL: **White Pass and Yukon Railroad**, depot at 1st Avenue

144

Pony-drawn depot wagon is taxi on Skagway's historic Broadway.

and Spring St., .3 miles from ferry. Information: White Pass and Yukon Route, Box 2147, Seattle, WA 98111. Closed.

AIR: **Skagway Air Service,** Box 357, Skagway 99840. 983-2233. **LAB Flying Service,** Juneau. **Wings of Alaska,** 983-2471.

ROAD: To Carcross and on to Whitehorse, open May 15 to September 15, at least. Gravel. Snow conditions often permit longer open season.

Note that Canadian and U.S. customs are closed near White Pass from midnight to 8 a.m. and there are no facilities nearby.

BAGGAGE STORAGE at hotels, for patrons, on day of departure. **Bunkhouse** also has storage for non-patrons, small charge.

HOTELS
(rates plus 6% tax)

Gold Rush Lodge—.7 mile from ferry, 6th and Alaska. Box 514, Skagway 99840. 983-2831. Street level. Modern. TV in rooms. Reservations advised. 12 rooms, Single $45, Double $55. Open May 1–Oct. 1.

Golden North—.35 mile from ferry, on Broadway and 3rd, Box 431, Skagway 99840. 983-2451. Restaurant, lounge, gift shop, tours. Single $60, Double $70–75, Triple $80, Quad $85. Has Gold Rush era furnishing.

Irene's Inn—.5 mile from ferry, on Broadway at 6th, Box 538, Skagway, 99840. 983-2520. Restaurant. Single $25, Double $30–40.

Klondike—.4 mile from ferry, 3rd Avenue between Broadway and Spring, Box 515, Skagway, 99840. (907) 983-2291. Restaurant and cocktail lounge. Rooms slightly larger than bed. Rates highest in town. Open summer only.

Skagway Inn—.55 mile from ferry, on Broadway between 6th and 7th, Box 129, Skagway 99840. (907) 983-2289. Living room. Single $35, Double $40, Triple $45, Quadruple $50. Add'l, $5/person. Winter weekly rates available. Built 1897. Gold Rush atmosphere.

Taiya Lodge—.6 mile from ferry, on 6th between Broadway and State, Box 101, Skagway, 99840. (907) 983-2414. 23 rooms, private and shared baths. With private baths, Single $47.70, Double $56.18, Triple $62.01, Quad $67.84. With shared baths, Single $31.80, Double $37.10, Triple $42.40, Quad $47.70. (1983 rates.) Summer only.

Fifth Avenue Bunkhouse—.37 mile from ferry downtown, on 5th between Broadway and State. Box 48, Skagway 99840. (907) 983-2568. Private cushioned bunks. Two bunks per cubicle. Bring sleeping bags. $10/person. Private redwood sauna, $5/person, $10 minimum. Showers and blankets available.

Wind Valley Lodge—.8 mile from ferry, 22nd and State Street. Box 354, Skagway 99840. 983-2236. Modern. TV in rooms. Reservations advised. Single $40, Double $46.

TRAILER PARKS

Karkross Kamper Kourt—1 mile, on 22nd between State and Main Streets. Large, modern facilities. Box 177, Skagway. 5 spaces with electricity and sewer. 30 spaces without hookups. Rates similar to Klondike Camper Court (below). Dump station.

Hoover's Camper Court—1/2 mile, 4th Ave., between State and Main Streets. Box 108, Skagway. (907) 983-2454. 12 spaces with hookups. $5 with electricity, $10 water, sewer, electricity. Hot showers.

CAMPGROUNDS

Hanousek Park—.9 mile from ferry, Broadway at 14th. 11 spaces, firepits, tables, water, restrooms. $5 vehicle space or tent site. Electrical hookup $2.50 add'l. Open May 15–October 1.

Liarsville State Campground—3 miles off Dyea Road after crossing river. 6 spaces. Fire pits, tables, pit toilets, wood. Free.

Pullen Creek Park & RV Campground—.2 mile from ferry, to right of Broadway. New city-owned campground. Some spaces with hookups. Park has a creek, pond, picnic shelter. $8 with water. $10.50 with water and electricity. Bathhouse with showers.

Dyea—9 miles. Unimproved, limited space. Picnicking, pit toilets.

FACILITIES

DUMP STATION: **Hanousek Park** and both trailer parks.

PROPANE: **Nova Warner**, 13th Ave., between State and Main.

DIESEL: **Service Unlimited**, International Chevron. 2nd and State Streets.

ICE: **Fairway Supermarket**, all liquor stores.

CLINIC: Dahl Clinic. 11th Ave., between State and Main. 9–5 weekdays, 983-2255. After hours, 983-2418.

PETS: Veterinarian is **Judy Selmer**, Broadway & 7th. 983-2313.

LAUNDROMAT

New facility at corner of 5th and Broadway. Dry cleaning, showers.

BOATS

Charters and boat tours. Information at National Park Service. Moorage and fuel available.

Cabin at Lake Lindeman on the Canadian part of the Chilkoot Trail. Here the gold seekers cut trees and built boats to continue down the Yukon River.

THE CHILKOOT PASS

Gold was discovered in creeks running into the Yukon's Klondike River in August 1896. As word spread through the north country, prospectors for many hundreds of miles around converged on the camp that became Dawson City. They staked claims, struggled and starved with bottles of gold nuggets on the shelf (there was gold but not enough food for so many people in the Yukon that winter). Finally in July 1897 the *Portland* arrived in Seattle with a load of gold, and the rush was on, world-wide.

Despite its difficulties, the Chilkoot Pass proved to be the quickest and one of the easiest routes to the Klondike. During the winter of 1897–98 thousands struggled over the pass, not once but many times as they shuttled back and forth moving the ton of supplies the Mounties now required for entry to the Yukon (to avoid a repetition of the starving times). By spring, when the ice went out on the river, over 20,000 miners waited on the shores of Lakes Lindeman and Bennett with hand-built boats to float the last 500 miles. They arrived to find all likely land and much unlikely area already staked. Few got any gold, but for all the trip was the most memorable time of their lives.

Today the trail is included in national parks on both sides of the border and maintained by U.S. and Canadian rangers. Many artifacts remain, and must be left as they lie. Along the trail are remains of wagons, boots, harnesses, stoves, and sleds once pulled by miners. There are metal pictures of views as they were then from the places you are standing now. The Chilkoot Trail is much more than a rugged 33-mile backpack trip. Even in summer it's a walk for several days through the world's most scenic historical museum.

To enjoy this trip requires some planning. The trail goes from sea level at Dyea to 3739 ft. at the summit, mostly in the last four miles (which are very hard on legs if you start from the north end and go in reverse), and back to 2153 ft. at Lake Bennett. July is the most popular month, as much of the winter's snow is gone and the wildflowers are lovely. The trip takes three to five days for most people.

You still can expect wind and rain any time. In the pass this can be miserable and force you to concentrate on the trail markers so as not to lose the trail. The trail is often muddy, crosses streams, has several miles of snow at any season and several miles of loose rock near the U.S. side of the pass. For latest conditions on the trail you should see the National Park Service in Skagway, which can give you a useful trail profile and the Canadian number to call for customs clearance. Topographic maps are available at the Skagway Sports Emporium on Fourth Avenue.

Adequate clothing and boots well broken-in are critical. The shelters are widely separated and nowhere near the pass. Good rain gear that's windproof is essential—rain pants and parka or cagoule. Ponchos don't work in wind, and the new breathable synthetics haven't proven waterproof in this climate for anyone I know. Pants *must* be wool or polyester fleece. Damp cotton pants lose heat, even under rain pants, faster than if you were undressed. Wearing them here leaves your whole safety margin to the luck of the weather and says some things about your judgment you wouldn't want to advertise. A wool cap and water repellent gloves that dry quickly are essential. Breathable gaiters are very good for keeping mud and snow out of boots, and keeping pants dry.

Camping is only approved in designated spots. Wood is scarce and you are advised to bring a stove and fuel for cooking. Shelters are only for drying out—not for camping in. You should also bring 50 feet of light rope for hauling your pack up out of bears' reach on the horizontal poles provided at most campsites. Deep Lake is the prettiest campsite on the trail but is located so it doesn't fit many people's schedules. Happy Camp is *not* in the first trees you come to on the Canadian side, and the "four miles" the map says from the summit are a sadistic underestimate. But this is a great trip and one I want to do again!

Returning from Bennett was easier when the train ran and you just had lunch and got on to go to Whitehorse or back to Skagway. Now your choices are: 1) skip Bennett and leave the trail at a fork just beyond Bare Loon Lake at about Mile 30 for a five-mile walk out the train tracks to a place on the road called Log Cabin where there's no longer a cabin, to meet the bus (get schedule in Skagway); 2) walk all the way to Bennett and then eight miles back on the tracks to Log Cabin, at least getting to see the whole historical story; or 3) if boats run on Bennett Lake, make reservations, and ride up from Bennett to Carcross (an interesting place to visit with museums and a restored lake steamer), taking the bus from there back to Skagway or on to Whitehorse. In 1983 we did that, paying $35 for the boat ride and $17 for the bus back to Skagway. The cost was why most people that summer walked out to Log Cabin. Boats are expected but not sure for summer 1985.

SMALLER PORTS
(Served by the *Aurora*, *Chilkat*, and *LeConte*, but not by the larger ferries)

METLAKATLA
(Area Code 907, Zip Code 99926)

MELAKATLA (pop. 1100) was established in 1887 when Father Duncan moved his religious community of Tsimshian Indians from Canada to Annette Island. The Island remains an Indian reservation, by vote, after the native claims settlement. A neat, well-planned community, Melakatla depends on timber and fishing, with both a cannery and a sawmill in town. The eastern half of the island is mountainous with lakes and waterfalls, while the western half, where the town and 7500 ft. airport are, is flat.

TO SEE AND DO

• See Father Duncan's Cottage, open 10–5, Mon.–Fri. Weekends by request. Restored as a museum. Curator, 886-6926.

• See cannery operating in season.

• See Duncan Memorial Church, replica of the original burned in 1948.

• See the longhouse, used for tribal ceremonies. Tsimshian crafts displayed and for sale.

• Beachcomb, picnic, hike almost anywhere on island. Walk out road west, past cemetery is popular. Pt. Davidson, 10 miles by gravel road, is good picnic and bird watching area. Purple Lake Trail, 3 miles, is steep and rugged, but beautiful.

151

• Bring bicycle on ferry for tour of island roads, trip to Pt. Davidson. Call Community Services Dept., Bonnie G. Scudero, or Stanley Patterson, 886-1216 for info.

• For the rugged, get let off (from Ketchikan or Metlakatla) by charter boat or plane on east side of island near Ham Island and backpack across, catching ferry back to Ketchikan.

• Founder's Day, Aug. 7. Celebrates arrival of Father Duncan and his followers in 1887. Tribal dancers, community lunch, special events.

• See operating fish hatchery at south end of the island.

• Walk trails such as Yellow Hill Viewpoint Trail, two miles south of town, and Skaters Lake Trail (1/2 mile long), 1/4 miles from town toward airport.

FACILITIES

ACCOMMODATIONS: **Taquan Inn Motel**, Metlakatla, AK 99926. (907) 886-7865. 8 double rooms. $30 per person, $50 with meals.

AIR SERVICE: **Taquan Air Service**, charter and regular service to Ketchikan. Box 600, Metlakatla. Jerry Scudero. (907) 886-6868, 6888.

CAR RENTAL: **Rent-A-Dent** in Metlakatla. Toll-free reservation from U.S. outside Washington, 1 (800) 426-5243. Metlakatla, 886-4622.

BUS SERVICE: None public.

GROCERY STORES: 1 supermarket, 1 minimart.

SWIMMING POOL, with sauna and fitness room, open to public at Lepquinum Recreation Center.

BOATS: Visiting boats and vehicles can get fuel at Guthries' on dock, tie up. A new breakwater and small boat harbor are completed.

FERRY: Ferry service is almost daily, 2 hours from Ketchikan on *Chilkat*. The ferry dock is 1/2 mile from downtown.

Note that the *Chilkat* makes three trips daily from Ketchikan Wed.–Sat. in 1985, so a very enjoyable day tour would be riding the early morning trip over to Metlakatla and the afternoon run back, leaving Ketchikan at 6:30 a.m. and returning at 6:20 p.m.

INFORMATION AVAILABLE at the Mayor's Office, 886-4868, or Community Services Dept., 886-1216, M–F 8–5. Very helpful people. The Community Services Dept. will be glad to help you. Box 458, Metlakatla 99926.

Note: Metlakatla is legally dry. There is no place to buy alcohol, and it cannot legally be brought to the island.

A drum seiner, seen in Canada but not Alaska, reels in its net.

Klawock's totem park, assembled during CCC days, overlooks harbor and fish processing plants.

PRINCE OF WALES ISLAND, CRAIG, KLAWOCK
(Area Code 907, Zip Codes Craig, 99921, Klawock 99925, Hydaburg 99922)

PRINCE OF WALES, largest island in Southeastern Alaska, 45 miles west of Ketchikan, is served by ferry to Hollis, several times weekly. From there a gravel road reaches Craig, 31 miles, pop. about 908, and Klawock, with another road to the big logging camp of Thorne Bay. Pt. Baker, also on the island, is reachable only by air and boat. Recent additions to the road system also now reach the logging camps of Whale Pass and Coffman Cove and the native fishing village of Hydaburg.

There is good fishing in many places, both fresh and saltwater. The west coast has many islands with sheltered coastline—a good place for boat touring and camping. Fishing and logging

154

are the main activities on the island. There is abundant wildlife, including many black bears and eagles.

TO SEE AND DO

• Visit totem park at Klawock, 21 totems.

• Fish, hunt, birdwatch many places, in season.

• Enjoy July 4th celebration in Craig—logging contests, etc.

• **Big** king salmon here. Fishing derby.

FACILITIES

ROADS: Most extensive road system in Southeastern Alaska, mostly gravel, though some in central part of island is now paved. Vehicles going to northern area should carry extra fuel and two spare tires. Watch for logging trucks. Hollis, a former logging camp, has no facilities.

ACCOMMODATIONS: **Haida Way Lodge**, downtown Craig, 31 miles from Hollis. On Front St., P.O. Box 90, Craig, 99921. (907) 826-3268. 16 units. TV, complimentary coffee, phones. Restaurant and lounge in summer. Open all year, Single and Double $53, with Kitchenette $63.

Fireweed Lodge, 30 miles from Hollis. On Hollis Hwy., P.O. Box 116, Klawock, 99925. (907) 755-2226. Courtesy car to Craig. Restaurant, open all year. Boats, canoes, fishing gear for rent. Salmon, steelhead, halibut, trout. Single $50, Double $75, with meals. Add'l, $10/person. Extended stay rates for over 7 days. Children under 5 free.

Karta Inn, small, rustic lodge near Hollis. Will pick up at Ferry. Marine radio telephone, "Darmy J. 2" through Ratz Mt. operator, David Gubser, Box 114, Craig 99921. Air charter from Ketchikan about $32. Rates include fishing aboard cruiser, all meals, home-baked bread, fresh seafood. Non-smokers 10% discount. Current rates unknown.

Prince of Wales Lodge, 26 miles from Hollis. On Big Salt Rd. P.O. Box 72, Klawock, 99925. (907) 755-2227. Operates package only. Others may use restaurant. Open 10 months a year.

Package tours start at $425 per person for three days, low season rate. Reservations office: 7320 6th Avenue #20, Tacoma, WA 98406. (206) 565-3629. (1984 rates).

Ruth Ann's Hotel, 31 miles from Hollis. P.O. Box 145, Craig 99921. (907) 826-3377. Restaurant and lounge. Single $40, Double $45.

SPORTS EQUIPMENT: **Log Cabin Sports Rental, Inc.**, 26 miles from ferry. P.O. Box 54, Klawock, 99925. (907) 755-2205. Has bicycles, tents, fishing equipment, showers, boats for rent separately or as package. Fishing and adventure packages, include halibut and salmon charters, gold panning, backpacking and canoeing, beach cabins or efficiency apartments, free transportation to and from ferry. Fishing packages including transportation from Ketchikan, boat and gear for four days/three nights: beach cabins with shared kitchen $445/person, efficiency apartments with kitchen, $470/person.

Log Cabin Sports Rental, six spaces with hookups, $20 per vehicle and two people.

TAXI between Hollis and Craig, Klawock. **Rainbow Cab**, Gen. Delivery, Craig 99921. 826-3473. Meets all ferries at Hollis. Most lodges have courtesy cars for their guests. **Prince of Wales Lodge** has a rental car. Sometimes it is possible to hitch rides with people driving off ferry or local people meeting passengers.

BUS SERVICE: to ferry **Hamilton Bus Service**, 826-3229.

CAR RENTAL: **Rent-A-Dent**, Klawock. 755-9000. Toll free outside of Washington: 1 (800) 426-5243.

GROCERY STORES: three in Craig, generally open 9 a.m. to 7 p.m., supermarket, beauty shop, clothing stores. Klawock has convenience store and a general store. Thorne Bay, Coffman Cove, Whale Pass and Hydaburg have small grocery stores.

RESTAURANTS: four in Craig (four in summer).

LAUNDROMAT: City Center, Craig. **Crystal Dairy** in Klawock.

GAS STATIONS in Craig, Klawock, Thorne Bay.

PROPANE and DIESEL: **Black Bear** in Klawock.

ICE: all grocery stores, most liquor stores.

HEALTH CLINIC: Craig, with doctor, health aide and public health nurse. Open 10–4, M–F. Radio contact with hospital in Ketchikan. 826-3257, after hours 826-3330.

BOAT FUEL: Craig and Thorne Bay (as a convenience here). Boat rentals at Thorne Bay. Launch ramp, Craig, at City Center (North Cove). Charters in Craig—check with City Hall or town bulletin boards.

CHARTER AIR SERVICE from Ketchikan by any of the operators there. **Tyee** and **Westflight** have scheduled service.

INFORMATION AVAILABLE at City Center, City of Craig, P.O. Box 23, Craig 99921. (907) 826-3275. Or U.S. Forest Service in Craig, or from Ketchikan Visitors' Bureau and U.S. Forest Service in Ketchikan. City of Klawock, P.O. Box 113, Klawock 99925. (907) 755-2261.

KAKE
(Area Code 907, Zip Code 99830)

KAKE (pop. 679) is a Tlingit Indian fishing village on Kupreanof Island, west of Petersburg. It is scenic, has some gravel logging roads, excellent fishing and is home of the world's tallest totem pole, 124½ feet tall, centerpiece of the Alaska pavilion at the 1970 World's Fair in Japan. Ferry dock 1½ miles from center of town.

TO SEE AND DO

• Fish anywhere, even at the ferry terminal, for halibut, king salmon, sole. Rainbow trout in streams.

157

- Hike, camp, beachcomb. Logging roads provide some trails and ski touring in winter. Road south leads short distance to Boot Lake picnic area, then on to Hamilton Bay, 20 miles.
- See the totem pole above town.
- Canoe or kayak in bay between Kupreanof and Kuiu Islands. Many inlets and small islands. Several Forest Service cabins.

FACILITIES

ACCOMMODATIONS: **New Town Inn**, P.O. Box 222, Kake. 785-3472. 1 mile from dock. Has 15 beds, sometimes full during construction season. Single $44, Double $66. Meals family style, for hotel guests only, $6 breakfast, $6 lunch, $12 dinner. (1984 rates).

RESTAURANTS: **Jackson's Coffee Shop**.

GROCERY STORES, 2.

BOAT FUEL available at Kake cannery dock, launch ramp. No charters or rentals.

PICNIC AREA at Portage Area, 1½ miles, to right of dock, no facilities.

TAXI: **Timber Wolf Cab**, 785-3875.

FERRY SERVICE from Petersburg, Sitka, and Juneau several times weekly, M/V LeConte.

AIR SERVICE: **Alaska Island Air**, daily from Petersburg. **Channel Flying** from Juneau.

INFORMATION: There is no Chamber of Commerce and Kake does not have pamphlets available. Petersburg Chamber of Commerce or U.S. Forest Service in Petersburg may have information. Kake City Hall, 785-3804.

ANGOON
(Area Code 907, Zip Code 99820)

ANGOON (pop. 562), is the only settlement on Admiralty Island. It is a Tlingit fishing village at the mouth of Mitchell Bay, a narrow-mouthed saltwater "chuck" featuring incredible currents at the tide change. This is also the end of the Cross-Admiralty canoe route, a system of cabins, trails, lakes and creeks, connecting the east and west sides of Admiralty Island. There is fishing in season for salmon, trout, herring and halibut. Most of this island has been declared a national monument. Check with U.S. Forest Service in Juneau, 789-3111. Wildlife watching is good—but note that this island has brown bears, an estimated average of one per square mile, who may regard a piece of stream or lakeshore as theirs.

TO SEE AND DO

• Fish, hike, beachcomb, canoe. Be careful of tides and rough water in Chatham Strait that can develop quickly. Weather can change rapidly.

• See Historical Center with new totems, artifacts, historical photos.

FACILITIES

FERRY SERVICE: Several times weekly from Juneau and Sitka.

CHARTER PLANE SERVICE from Juneau and Sitka. **Channel Flying Service** has mail run, 6 days a week from Juneau. **Bel Air Service** from Sitka, six days a week.

ACCOMMODATIONS: **Kootznahoo Inlet Lodge**, Box 134, Angoon, 788-3501. At plane float, 2 miles from dock. 10 units, 3 with kitchen. Restaurant. Single $55, Double $65, Triple $80. Add'l, $6/person. Laundry facilities. Skiff charters, $50–$150/day. Bring own fishing gear.

Raven Beaver Lodge, c/o Delores Starr, Manager, Box 67, Angoon, 99820. 788-3601. Three miles from dock. Baggage storage until checkout. All rooms have cooking facilities. Single $51. Add'l, $10.20/person.

Dick Powers Bed and Breakfast, Box 101, Angoon, 99820. (907) 788-3123.

GROCERY STORES: Two. Seaside and Angoon Trading Company.

BOAT FUEL at Angoon Standard Oil.

BOAT RENTALS, **Alaska Discovery** through Dick Powers, 788-3123.

CRAFTS: The villagers make and sell blankets, moccasins, and other beaded items at their homes.

LAUNDRY FACILITIES at hotels, coin operated.

TAXI: **Central Taxi, 788-3994.**

ICE: at the grocery stores.

INFORMATION AVAILABLE at the Angoon City Office, 788-3653 and 788-3663. P.O. Box 189, Angoon. Or at U.S. Nat'l. Monument Office, Community Services Building, 788-3166.

TENAKEE SPRINGS
(Area Code 907, Zip Code 99841)

TENAKEE SPRINGS (pop. 141) is a settlement near Tenakee Hot Springs on Chichagof Island. It is scenic, quiet, and marks one end of a good canoe route from Hoonah. Main street is a path. The only "cars" in town are the oil truck and fire truck. Hot springs feed the bath house adjacent to the dock and Main Street. The ferry dock is in the center of town. There are 16 miles of excellent footpath along the shoreline, extending 8 miles east and west of town.

Tenakee's waterfront caught the full force of a storm Thanksgiving Day, 1984, with a record high tide and waves plus 80 knot winds. A dozen buildings on pilings were lost and more were damaged by floating wreckage from adjacent houses. Part of the main street path was washed away, leaving some of the village without fire protection as the engine couldn't get there. Many people were homeless, camped in the school.

The following day, while state and federal officials declared a disaster and the National Guard mustered to clear smashed buildings off the beach, Tenakee appealed on Juneau radio for owners of hydraulic jacks to loan them so the people could jack salvageable houses back up on pilings before more high tides. The U.S. Coast Guard had agreed to fly the jacks over by helicopter. The ferry *Aurora* had already left all the trailer jacks she could spare when she stopped. It was an Alaskan solution—doing for themselves!

TO SEE AND DO

• Fish, hike, canoe. Salmon, halibut, trout.

• Enjoy hot mineral springs in Tenakee Bathhuse, next to ferry dock. Donations accepted to help maintain building.

FACILITIES

ACCOMMODATIONS: **Snyder Mercantile Co.**, P.O. Box 505, Tenakee Springs, 99841. 736-2205. Cottages for rent, with cooking facilities. Supplies available at Snyder's General Store. Near ferry dock and plane float. Cottages from $25/day, weekly rates Jan.–April. Cabins sleep 2–3. Reservations a must. Customers should bring own sleeping bags and check in at store 9 a.m.–5 p.m. Mon.–Sat. Closed Sun. If coming on ferry which arrives in the middle of the night, plan to camp out until store opens. Or arrive by plane in day and depart by ferry. Pets allowed.

Tenakee Bed and Breakfast, 1/4 mile from ferry. Mailing address: 167 S. Franklin, Juneau, 99801. Scheduled to open April 1985. Bar, housekeeping units. Closed Jan.–March. Single $45, Double $50.

CAMPGROUND at Indian River, 2 miles east of town. No facilities. Brown bears sometimes. Be careful with food and garbage and don't argue with the bears.

RESTAURANT: **Blue Moon Cafe** next to dock. **Tenakee Tavern and Bar**, beverages and pool tables.

GROCERY STORE adjacent to dock, open 9 a.m.–5 p.m. Mon.–Sat.

PUBLIC PHONE in booth near store and bath house. Available 24 hours/day. Phone is coinless. Accepts collect, credit card or 3rd party calls only.

BOAT FUEL and tie space available. A Juneau friend cautions boaters to tie near cafe carefully. He moored a skiff to the dock and failed to allow for its tidal swing. When he used the open-bottom restroom at the back of the cafe, he thought a skiff underneath looked familiar. It was!

BOAT CHARTER: **D&L Enterprises**, c/o Glenn Lockhart, Box 563, Tenakee Springs, 99841. (907) 736-2229. Fishing charters and transportation for hunters and campers.

FERRY SERVICE: twice from Juneau and Sitka, northbound Thursday and Sunday, Southbound Friday. From Juneau, leaving Friday afternoon and returning Sunday morning, this is a nice excursion. People in Tenakee have become sensitive to gawkers with cameras tramping through their yards, etc. Please be considerate.

CHARTER AIR SERVICE: operators in Juneau and Sitka. **Channel Flying** has the mail run, 6 days a week.

INFORMATION AVAILABLE, Snyder Mercantile Co. P.O. Box 505, Tenakee Springs, AK 99841.

HOONAH
(Area Code 907, Zip Code 99829)

HOONAH (pop. 1000) is the site of a very old Tlingit settlement on Port Frederick, a good natural harbor that remained ice-free during the last glacial advance that filled Glacier Bay only 200 years ago. Fishing and subsistence are the main activities. It has very frequent ferry service from Juneau. On the north shore of Chichagof Island, it is at one end of the canoe route to Tenakee Springs.

TO SEE AND DO

• Walk around the scenic village with its beautiful views across Port Frederick.

• Hike Spasski Trail, 3½ miles, east of town.

• Enjoy the Hoonah Indian Association Culture Center at end of Roosevelt Drive, 9–4:30, Mon.–Fri. Possibly weekends in summer. 945-3600. From town center, it's up the hill.

• Walk the road to the left (northwest) of the ferry dock to the picturesque old cannery at its end. Fishing is good for Dolly Varden from the point. Beach north of cannery has a fascinating variety of banded pebbles and rocks.

• Fish for salmon, trout, halibut.

FACILITIES
(rates plus 3% tax)

ACCOMMODATIONS: **Totem Lodge**, Box 320ip, Hoonah, 99829. (907) 945-3636. 28 rooms, dining room, lounge, TV. Fishing and hunting charters. Single $50, Double $65. Add'l, $10/person.

Dliet Toos Cafe and Inn, 1/2 mile from ferry, Front Street, P.O. Box 378, Hoonah, 99829. (907) 945-3228. Restaurant, coffee shop, bar. Housekeeping units available. Open all year. Single, $45, Double, $55.

CAMP: Check with harbormaster, Paul Dybdahl for acceptable place. 945-3670.

GROCERY STORES: There are 3.

BUS: none.

TAXI: none.

FERRY SERVICE: dock about 1 mile from center of town.

AIRPORT: 3600 ft. runway, gravel, lighted, soon to be paved. Scheduled air service from Juneau, **LAB Flying Service**, **Channel Flying Service**, and **Wings of Alaska**.

BOAT FUEL: Union and Standard available. Tie-up space.

FISHING GUIDE SERVICE: Check with Totem Lodge.

BOAT CHARTER: **Double Eagle Charters**, c/o Ernest Jack, Box 94, Hoonah 99829. (907) 945-3253. Sport fishing for up to

6 passengers. Gear and bait provided. **Mt. Fairweather Charters,** c/o Richard G. Dalton, Sr., Box 154, Hoonah 99829. (907) 945-3302. Charter fishing and sightseeing. Overnight stays in family-owned cabins.

INFORMATION AVAILABLE, City Hall M–F, 945-3664. Miles Murphy, Mayor, is very helpful. Mike Tavoliero, City Manager.

HAPPENINGS

Kids' Trout Derby, end of April and first week of May.

Kids' Field Day, third week of May, end-of-school games, races. Fishing contest.

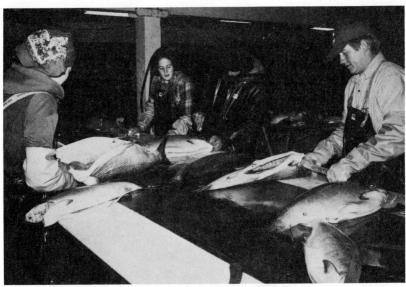

Workers prepare salmon to be frozen whole in Pelican Cold Storage plant.

PELICAN
(Area Code 907, Zip Code 99832)

PELICAN, pop. 213, is a tiny fishing village with a cold storage plant on Lisianski Inlet, a scenic fiord on the northwest corner of Chichagof Island. Ferry service is once a month all year, and the ferry only stays 2 hours, but that is time to get off (and plan to fly back to Juneau) or walk up the one-lane boardwalk main street to the far end of town. Sometimes fish or crab can be bought from the cold storage plant. It is a bustling place during fishing season or on 4th of July, the big annual date in town. The round trip on the ferry makes a good one day excursion from Juneau, stopping at Hoonah both ways in summer. In 1985 the ferry goes several times each month May through September.

TO SEE AND DO

• Walk around town, including fishing harbor with lots of gear, types of boats. Few places in America have this lifestyle in the 20th century.

• Fish anywhere.

• Kayak scenic West Chichagof Island if you've solved the problem of how to move the boat the non-ferry direction from Juneau, or can stay until ferry's next trip. Some experienced paddlers go from Pelican to Sitka.

FACILITIES

ACCOMMODATIONS: **Rosie's Bar & Grill**, 100 yds. from ferry dock, has four rooms for rent. P.O. Box 783, Pelikan 99832. (907) 735-2265. Rooms adjacent to Rosie's. Gift shop and museum. $65 per room, single or double. Open all year.

CAMPING: Ask the locals. Very little level ground in the area. The flats across the creek south of town flood at high tide.

GROCERY STORE: 1 (general store).

RESTAURANT: One restaurant, two bar & grills.

BOAT FUEL at Chevron in center of town. No rentals or charters.

LAUNDROMAT: downtown.

CHARTER AIR SERVICE available from Juneau and Sitka. **Channel Flying** in 1985 has the mail run, 6 days a week, no Sundays, from Juneau. Seat rate at press time is $72. The same flight also serves Elfin Cove, a smaller village a few miles north, at the same fare.

INFORMATION AVAILABLE City of Pelican, Box 757, Pelican 99832, 735-2202.

HAVING FUN, WITHOUT ACCIDENT, OFF THE BEATEN TRACK

Southeastern Alaska is a big area with few people and lots of cool, wet weather, poor visibility, and miles of **very cold** water. One quickly develops respect for prehistoric Indians who roamed these forests and paddled open canoes as far as Portland, Oregon. They must have been very good at staying dry, or very stoic about being cold and wet.

Judgment and planning are everything, whether you are hiking, boating, or flying. Any time you move into a new climate and an unfamiliar area, you have a new set of nature's rules to learn, and in Alaska, nature can be very quick and violent.

Weather, tides, and currents change rapidly here. When 20 vertical feet of water go somewhere every 6 hours, the currents in narrow places, especially mouths of wider bays, can quickly get over 8 knots. Winds and downdrafts in mountain passes can do the same thing. Visibility can drop rapidly, a long way from harbor, airport, or campsite.

Clothing should include the rain gear and warm woolens you'll need if it gets cold and wet. If it's warm, you can wear light clothing but have the other with you. Passengers in the author's plane wear a lifejacket or floatcoat flying over water, and wear or bring boots, parka, etc. for flying over the icefield. If a boat sinks or capsizes, what will you have with you on the beach? Down is useless when wet—wool and fiberfill retain some warmth. Wet blue jeans are deadly. Surplus stores and the Salvation Army have inexpensive wool pants.

Shelter. Some light emergency shelter should be in the boat, plane or pack, adequate for overnight in rain on wet ground. A tube tent fastened to the floatcoat or lifejacket, so it and you reach shore together, is a good idea.

Fire starter or stove can be useful, though it's best not to count on being able to burn wet wood. Large, clear plastic playing dice make excellent fire starter that doesn't crumble in a pocket. Bring an ample supply of starter and dry matches. Practice starting fires in wet conditions if you haven't done it before. Spruce sap or gum pulled off tree trunks was used by natives as fire starter.

Distress signals and extra food are a must. People are hard to see in this big country, and it helps to make it easy for those looking for you. Pocket flares or a strobe are good and don't weigh much. Carry a copy of the air-to-ground emergency signals. Waving OK to a plane or helicopter could send him off when you need him.

Let someone know where you are going, and don't go alone. You would want someone to look for you, wouldn't you? The smaller the area they have to search, the sooner you'll be in where it's dry and warm. Do let people know when you've returned. Stay together.

Bears need respect if we are to coexist. Brown bears, especially, can claim a territory or fishing stream as theirs. Keep food and food smells away from camp and out of pockets. Burn all garbage. Make some noise anywhere you go. Bears are apparently attracted to human menstrual odors. Ask local people about recent bear activity. Anything a bear takes is now *his*.

Turn back if weather or sea get bad. Check weather before going, and then watch it. Listen for reports if you have radio. Weather can change very rapidly here.

Don't HAVE TO get there, or back today. Hole up and wait it out. Bring what you'll need to do that.

Learn the area as soon as possible, carry charts, and ask the locals a lot of questions. Many aviation radio repeaters have recently been installed in Southeast Alaska. With current charts, you can talk to FSS in Ketchikan, Sitka, or Juneau from most areas even if you are below hilltops.

For pilots and boaters: In air or water, know the rules of the road and obey. Know your equipment and your ability. Always have an alternate goal—not easy when bays or airports are far apart. Don't overload—always have a margin. Carry adequate personal flotation gear, and wear it when the sea is rough. Watch for partly submerged logs and ice.

Work up to bigger things; don't just jump in. A hiker on his first backpack trip ever, on Chilkoot Pass, complained to the ranger about the steep trail. "But didn't the pictures in town show you it would be steep?" "Oh, I thought with all the people going over, it would have worn down some."

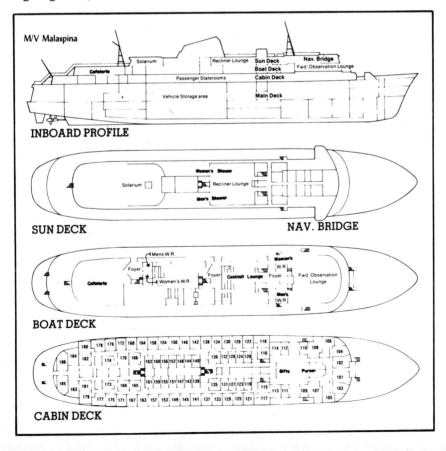

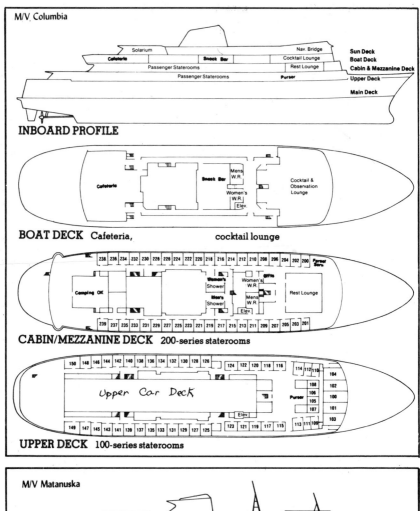

M/V. Columbia

Solarium
Nav. Bridge — Sun Deck
Cafeteria — Snack Bar — Cocktail Lounge — Boat Deck
Passenger Staterooms — Rest Lounge — Cabin & Mezzanine Deck
Passenger Staterooms — Purser — Upper Deck
Main Deck

INBOARD PROFILE

Cafeteria — Snack Bar — Mens W.R. — Women's W.R. — Elev. — Cocktail & Observation Lounge

BOAT DECK Cafeteria, cocktail lounge

238 236 234 232 230 228 226 224 222 220 218 216 214 212 210 208 206 204 202 200 | Purser Serv.
Camping OK — Women's Shower — Men's Shower — Women's W.R. — Gifts — Mens W.R. — Elev. — Rest Lounge
239 237 235 233 231 229 227 225 223 221 219 217 215 213 211 209 207 205 203 201

CABIN/MEZZANINE DECK 200-series staterooms

150 148 146 144 142 140 138 136 134 132 130 128 126 | 124 122 120 118 116 | 114 112 110 | 104
108 | 102
Upper Car Deck — Purser — 106 105 | 100
107 | 101
Elev.
149 147 145 143 141 139 137 135 133 131 129 127 125 | 123 121 119 117 115 | 113 111 109 | 103

UPPER DECK 100-series staterooms

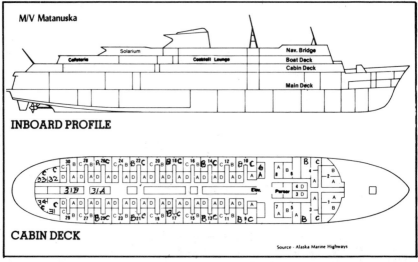

M/V Matanuska

Solarium
Nav. Bridge
Cafeteria — Cocktail Lounge — Boat Deck
Cabin Deck
Main Deck

INBOARD PROFILE

CABIN DECK

Source - Alaska Marine Highways

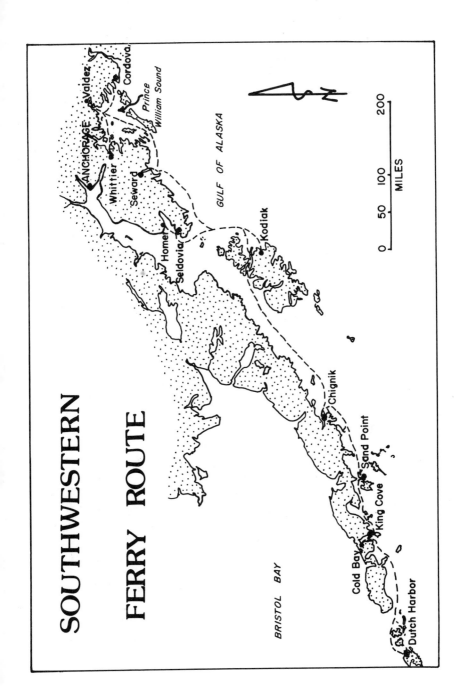

SOUTHWESTERN

FERRY ROUTE

BRISTOL BAY

GULF OF ALASKA

ANCHORAGE
Valdez
Cordova
Prince
William Sound
Whittier
Seward
Homer
Seldovia
Kodiak
Chignik
Sand Point
King Cove
Cold Bay
Dutch Harbor

N

0   50   100   200
MILES

THE SOUTHWESTERN FERRY SYSTEM

The two ferries, *Bartlett* and *Tustamena*, comprise the Southwest System, also part of the Alaska Marine Highway. The routes don't connect with the Southeastern system, though the *Tustamena* makes several stops in Southeastern Alaska on her annual trip to the shipyard in Seattle. The *Bartlett* serves Prince William Sound with stops at Whittier, Valdez, and Cordova. The *Tustamena* serves Seward, Seldovia, Homer, Kodiak, Port Lions (on Kodiak Island), Valdez and Cordova, and has four trips annually out the Aleutian Chain with stops both ways at Kodiak, Chignik, Sand Point, King Cove, Cold Bay and Dutch Harbor. **Reservations** are needed, even for walk-on passengers on all these runs, especially in summer.

The *Bartlett*'s trips in Prince William Sound are beautifully scenic and make a good excursion from Anchorage, using the Alaska Railroad to reach the ferry at Whittier, which does not have road access. One can also drive to or from Valdez, which has bus service as well. Cordova does not have road connections with the rest of Alaska, though it has daily service from Anchorage and Juneau with **Alaska Airlines**. The nearby Copper River Delta is one of the world's important migratory waterfowl rest areas and also has nesting swans.

The *Bartlett* turns into the fiord and cruises near Columbia Glacier for an hour between Valdez and Whittier on Wednesdays, Fridays, Saturday and Sunday, May 14 to Sept. 17, 1985. The officers note otters and seals on the ice. As the huge front of the glacier is very active, you are sure to see pieces "calve off" into the bay and feel the waves. On weekends there is also a Forest Service naturalist aboard helping you spot wildlife. Whether you ride the ferry or one of the cruise boats between Valdez, this is one of the most memorable experiences in Alaska!

In the summer of 1985 the *Tustamena* will stop near the Columbia Glacier on seven weekend trips between Seward and Valdez, allowing some who aren't going to Whittier a glacier view.

The *Tustamena*'s runs to Kodiak Island are an experience. These are not protected "inside" waters, and are locally known as the "Dramamine run." If you want the experience or want to get your car to Kodiak, you can enjoy a real ocean trip. For the runs out the Chain you definitely need reservations. The *Tustamena* has some staterooms (the *Bartlett* has none).

If you are going on the May, June, July, or September trips out the Chain, most direct access is from Homer. If you get on the ferry at Seward, the ferry goes to Kodiak and back to Homer, then back to Seward, before going west. You can stay on for the three crossings of the Gulf, paying for the additional distance for the stateroom, or you can stop over at Kodiak. For the trips west or to Kodiak, you could go one way on the ferry and fly by airline to or from Anchorage in the other direction. Kodiak has famous scenery, sportfishing (and one of the biggest commercial fishing fleets in the world), and hunting. Besides fishing and hunting and weather you will want to dress well for, the towns on the Alaska Peninsula and the Aleutian Chain are famous for birdwatching during migration. (Also famous is the Copper River Delta near Cordova.) Whole species of waterfowl pass through here, stopping off to rest and feed at eelgrass beds in Izembek Lagoon near Cold Bay.

During the winter of 1984–85 the *Tustamena* made several trips between Seward and Juneau on an experimental basis. If these continue, not announced yet, in winter they would give an alternative to driving the highway. A smooth ride is not guaranteed across the Gulf of Alaska in winter! In any later winter, the *Tustamena* makes a round trip from Seward to Seattle, stopping in Juneau, when she goes to shipyard, carrying passengers and vehicles. These trips are reserved far in advance.

The Southwest ferries both have solariums and dining rooms with service, but neither has elevators. The *Bartlett* does not have rental blankets or pillows (most of its runs are in daylight) or a baggage cart. In some cases the terminal buildings are a hundred yards or more from the ship, so boarding is a bit more strenuous for the elderly or handicapped than on the Southeastern ships. For another dimension to Alaska and scenery that can't be beat, why not try the marine buses of the Southwest?

M.V. Tustumena

MAY 1 - MAY 11			DUTCH HARBOR TRIPS
SUN	LV SEWARD	8:30 PM	MAY 12 - 19
MON	LV PORT LIONS	10:15 AM	JUNE 9 - 16
MON	LV KODIAK	3:00 PM	JULY 7 - 14
TUE	LV HOMER	2:30 AM	SEPTEMBER 15 - 22
TUE	AR SELDOVIA	4:00 AM	
TUE	LV SELDOVIA	5:15 AM	SUN LV SEWARD 1:30 PM
TUE	LV HOMER	8:30 AM	MON LV PORT LIONS 3:00 PM
TUE	AR KODIAK	6:15 PM	MON LV KODIAK 6:30 AM
TUE	LV KODIAK	9:00 PM	MON LV HOMER 6:00 PM
TUE	LV PORT LIONS	11:30 PM	MON AR SELDOVIA 7:30 PM
WED	LV HOMER	11:45 AM	MON LV SELDOVIA 8:15 PM
WED	AR SELDOVIA	1:15 PM	MON LV HOMER 11:45 PM
WED	LV SELDOVIA	4:30 PM	TUE LV KODIAK 12:45 PM
WED	LV HOMER	8:15 PM	WED LV CHIGNIK 7:45 AM
THU	LV KODIAK	8:15 AM	WED LV SAND POINT 6:15 PM
THU	LV SEWARD	11:45 PM	THU LV KING COVE 1:30 AM
FRI	LV CORDEZ	12:30 PM	THU LV COLD BAY 4:00 AM
FRI	AR VALDEZ	6:00 PM	THU AR DUTCH HARBOR 6:45 PM
FRI	LV VALDEZ	7:15 PM	THU LV DUTCH HARBOR 9:00 PM
SAT	LV CORDOVA	2:15 AM	FRI LV COLD BAY 12:45 PM
SAT	AR SEWARD	1:45 PM	FRI LV KING COVE 3:15 PM
			FRI LV SAND POINT 10:00 PM
			SAT LV CHIGNIK 8:00 AM
			SUN LV KODIAK 4:15 AM
			SUN AR SEWARD 5:30 PM

MAY 19 - JUNE 2		JUNE 2 - JUNE 9
JUNE 16 - JUNE 30		JUNE 30 - JULY 7
JULY 14 - SEPTEMBER 8		SEPTEMBER 8 - SEPTEMBER 15
SEPTEMBER 22 - SEPTEMBER 29		

			SUN LV SEWARD	8:30 PM
SUN	LV SEWARD	8:30 PM	MON LV PORT LIONS	10:15 AM
MON	LV PORT LIONS	10:15 AM	MON LV KODIAK	3:00 PM
MON	LV KODIAK	3:00 PM	TUE LV HOMER	2:30 AM
TUE	LV HOMER	2:30 AM	TUE AR SELDOVIA	4:00 AM
TUE	AR SELDOVIA	4:00 AM	TUE LV SELDOVIA	5:15 AM
TUE	LV SELDOVIA	5:15 AM	TUE LV HOMER	8:30 AM
TUE	LV HOMER	8:30 AM	TUE AR KODIAK	6:15 PM
TUE	AR KODIAK	6:15 PM	TUE LV KODIAK	9:00 PM
TUE	LV KODIAK	9:00 PM	TUE LV PORT LIONS	11:30 PM
TUE	LV PORT LIONS	11:30 PM	WED LV HOMER	11:45 AM
WED	LV HOMER	11:45 AM	WED AR SELDOVIA	1:15 PM
WED	AR SELDOVIA	1:15 PM	WED LV SELDOVIA	4:30 PM
WED	LV SELDOVIA	4:30 PM	WED LV HOMER	8:15 PM
WED	LV HOMER	8:15 PM	THU LV KODIAK	8:15 AM
THU	LV KODIAK	8:15 AM	THU. AR SEWARD	9:30 PM
THU	AR SEWARD	9:30 PM	FRI LV SEWARD	9:30 PM
FRI	LV SEWARD	10:30 PM	via Columbia Glacier	
via Columbia Glacier			SAT LV VALDEZ	10:30 AM
SAT	LV VALDEZ	1:30 PM	SAT AR CORDOVA	4:00 PM
SAT	AR CORDOVA	7:00 PM	SAT LV CORDOVA	4:45 PM
SAT	LV CORDOVA	10:45 PM	SAT LV VALDEZ**	11:00 PM
SUN	LV VALDEZ	5:30 AM	SUN AR SEWARD	10:00 AM
via Columbia Glacier			** Glacier will not be seen	
SUN	AR SEWARD	5:30 PM	at night	

M.V. Bartlett

MAY 14 - SEPTEMBER 17 at 5:30 AM		
TUE	LV CORDOVA	11:45 P
WED	LV VALDEZ	7:30 A
WED	AR WHITTIER	2:15 P
WED	LV WHITTIER	3:00 P
WED	LV VALDEZ	11:45 P
THU	AR CORDOVA	5:30 A
THU	LV CORDOVA	11:45 P
FRI	LV VALDEZ	7:30 A
FRI	AR WHITTIER	2:15 P
FRI	LV WHITTIER	3:00 P
FRI	AR VALDEZ	10:00 P
SAT	LV VALDEZ	7:30 A
SAT	AR WHITTIER	2:15 P
SAT	LV WHITTIER	3:00 P
SAT	AR VALDEZ	10:00 P
SUN	LV VALDEZ	7:30 A
SUN	AR WHITTIER	2:15 P
SUN	LV WHITTIER	3:00 P
SUN	AR VALDEZ	10:00 P
MON	LV VALDEZ	7:30 A
MON	AR WHITTIER	2:15 P
MON	LV WHITTIER	3:00 P
MON	LV VALDEZ	11:45 P
TUE	AR CORDOVA	5:30 A

MAY 1 - MAY 14
M.V. BARTLETT NOT IN SERVICE

SEPTEMBER 17 - 30		
TUE	LV CORDOVA	8:30 A
TUE	AR VALDEZ	2:15 P
WED	LV VALDEZ	8:30 A
WED	AR CORDOVA	2:15 P
THU	LV CORDOVA	8:30 A
THU	AR VALDEZ	2:15 P
FRI	LV VALDEZ	8:30 A
FRI	AR CORDOVA	2:15 P

Southeastern Offices—Skagway (907) 983-2941, Haines (907) 766-2111, Sitka (907) 747-8767, Petersburg (907) 772-3855, Wrangell (907) 874-3711, Ketchikan (907) 225-6181, Juneau (907) 465-3941, Prince Rupert (604) 627-1744.

SOUTHWESTERN OFFICES

ANCHORAGE	BOX 102344, ANCHORAGE, AK 99510	(907) 272-4482
CORDOVA	BOX 1247, CORDOVA, AK 99574	(907) 424-7333
SEWARD	BOX 66, SEWARD, AK 99664	(907) 224-5485
VALDEZ	BOX 647, VALDEZ, AK 99686	(907) 835-4436
HOMER	BOX 355, HOMER, AK 99603	(907) 235-8449
KODIAK	BOX 1592, KODIAK, AK 99615	(907) 486-3800
SELDOVIA	BOX 226, SELDOVIA, AK 99663	(907) 234-7868

THE AUTHOR

ELLEN SEARBY worked on the Alaska ferries as shipboard naturalist for the U.S. Forest Service during the summers 1975–77. Since 1978 she has worked as part of the ferry crew. Answering questions for many thousands of passengers, she learned what the Inside Passage traveler wanted and needed to know—and wrote it in this book.

She has worked in winter as a research analyst in Alaska's coastal management office. With an M.A. in geography from Stanford, a long-time interest in mountaineering ("I climbed with a lot of good people on their days off"), and a commercial pilot's license she uses to fly her 1948 Luscombe in Alaska and to California, she finds the Inside Passage a challenging place to be. In her spare time, she started SEADOGS, the Southeastern Alaska search and avalanche dog team. She and her dog now work independently.

In 1985 she completed research and writing, and published *The Costa Rica Traveler*.

Books from Windham Bay Press:
Box 1332, Juneau, Alaska 99802

The Inside Passage Traveler, Getting Around in Southeastern Alaska, 8th edition, by Ellen Searby. Photos, maps, 176 pages. Alaska! See more/spend less! Tells all you need to know to plan any kind of trip you want in the Inside Passage. This handy guide completely explains how to make the most of the Alaska ferry system, lists all the facilities in Southeast Alaska and Prince Rupert, B.C., with their prices, from deluxe hotels to cabins and youth hostels. Easy to read and use, with no paid advertising to weigh down your purse or pack. Enjoy a vacation according to your personal interests on this beautiful coast. $7.95 ppd surface, add $1.50 for air or $2 for foreign orders except Canada. ISBN 0-9605526-6-9.

The Costa Rica Traveler, Getting Around in Costa Rica, 1st edition, by Ellen Searby. Photos, maps, 208 pages. Enjoy this peaceful, tropical Camelot with its friendly people, miles of uncrowded beaches, tropical rain forest, volcanoes, and jungle waterways. Visit the country that has 1/10th of the world's bird species, over 850, over 1200 species of orchids alone, altitudes from Atlantic and Pacific Oceans to over 12,000 feet, all in an area the size of West Virginia! Here is some of the world's best deep-sea fishing, snorkeling, river rafting—all at reasonable cost. Hotels, facilities and sights are clearly explained so you can make your choices. $9.95 ppd surface, add $1.50 for air or $2.50 for foreign orders except Canada. ISBN 0-9605526-5-0.

Windham Bay Press, Box 1332, Juneau, Alaska 99802

	Quantity	Price*	Amount
_____	*The Inside Passage Traveler*	$7.95	_____
_____	*The Costa Rica Traveler*	9.95	_____
	Air or foreign postage:		
each	*Inside Passage Traveler*, $1.50 air, $2 foreign except Canada		_____
each	*Costa Rica Traveler*, $1.50 air, $2.50 foreign except Canada		_____
	Total in U.S. funds. Check okay if drawn on U.S. bank. No CODs or credit cards, please. Surface mail to East Coast from Alaska can take six weeks.		_____

Name _____

Address _____

City _____ State/Prov. _____ Zip _____

Country _____

*surface postage paid